MOBILIZING
~ FOR ~
# MISSION

12 LESSONS ON SPIRIT-EMPOWERED MISSIONS
~ TAUGHT IN ACTS 1:8 CONFERENCES ACROSS AFRICA ~

Denzil R. Miller

Mobilizing for Mission: 12 Lessons on Spirit-Empowered Missions: Taught in Acts 1:8 Conferences Across Africa. © 2019, Denzil R. Miller. © 2019, AIA Publications. All rights reserved. No part of this book may be reproduced, stored in a retrieval system, or transmitted in any form or by any means—electronic, mechanical, photocopy, recording, or otherwise—without prior written permission of the copyright owner, except brief quotations used in connection with reviews in magazines or newspapers.

All Scripture quotations in this book, unless otherwise indicated, are from the Holy Bible, English Standard Version® (ESV®) Copyright © 2001 by Crossway, a publishing ministry of Good News Publishers.

Scripture quotations marked NIV are taken from the Holy Bible, New International Version®, NIV®. Copyright © 1973, 1978, 1984 by Biblica, Inc.™ Used by permission of Zondervan.

Scripture quotations marked NASB are taken from the New American Standard Bible® Copyright © 1960, 1962, 1963, 1968, 1971, 1972, 1973, 1975, 1977, 1995 by the Lockman Foundation

Library of Congress Cataloging-in-Publication Data
Miller, Denzil R., 1946–

Mobilizing for Mission: 12 Lessons on Spirit-Empowered Missions: Taught in Acts 1:8 Conferences Across Africa / Denzil R. Miller

ISBN: 978-0-9997032-3-6

1. Bible. 2. Practical Theology 3. Pentecostal. 4. Leadership. 5. Missions

Printed in the United States of America
© 2019 Denzil R. Miller
© 2019 AIA Publications, Springfield, MO, USA

A Decade of Pentecost Publication
E-mail: ActsinAfrica@agmd.org
Websites: www.DecadeofPentecost.org
           www.ActsinAfrica.org
           www.DenzilRMiller.com

"But you will receive

Power

when the Holy Spirit has come upon you,
and you will be my

Witnesses

in Jerusalem and in all Judea and Samaria,
and to the ends of the earth."

~ Acts 1:8 ~

Table of Contents

Acknowledgement 7
Introduction 9

1. The Holy Spirit and the Mission of God 13
2. Spirit Baptism Revisited 23
3. What It Means to Be Pentecostal 33
4. Prayer and Pentecostal Revival 49
5. Planting the Spirit-Empowered Missionary Church 59
6. Leading a Church into Pentecostal Revival 71
7. How to Preach on the Baptism in the Holy Spirit 83
8. Praying with Believers to Receive the Holy Spirit 99
9. Pentecost and the Next Generation 111
10. Women and Pentecostal Revival 123
11. The Pentecostal Bible School 135
12. The Pentecostal Leader 145

Appendices:

    (1) Acts 1:8 Conference Planning Guide 159

    (2) Acts 1:8 Conference Prayer Guide 163

    (3) Strategy Sessions Guide 169

    (4) Sermon Outlines for Acts 1:8 Conferences 177

    (5) Typical Acts 1:8 Conference Schedules 185

Other Decade of Pentecost Books 187

ACKNOWLEDGEMENT

AIA Team (left to right): Denzil R. Miller, Sandy Miller, Enson M. Lwesya, and Mark R. Turney

I would be remiss if I failed to acknowledge the significant contribution others have made in the development of this book. Special recognition goes to the following Acts in Africa Initiative team members:

~ Mark R. Turney ~
~ Enson M. Lwesya ~
~ Sandy Miller ~

Certain lessons in this book were originally developed by these individuals and taught in Acts 1:8 Conferences across Africa. I have indicated these lessons with footnotes at the beginning of each chapter. Those lessons that are not footnoted were developed by me.

In the conferences, team members typically taught their own lessons. However, when the need arose, members would step up and teach one another's lessons. When we did this, we almost always spoke from the original developer's outline. We, of course, added our own unique insights on the topic. Through this process, we all gained a greater understanding of the subject being taught. In addition, we frequently sat and discussed the concepts contained in these lessons.

Acknowledgement

In time, it became almost impossible to separate one team member's insights from the others.

Though I wrote the book alone, in a very real sense, it has been a team effort. I therefore freely acknowledge that this work is as much theirs as it is mine.

~ Dr. Denzil R. Miller
Director
Acts in Africa Initiative

INTRODUCTION

For more than a decade, I have been privileged to work with some of the world's most gifted and visionary Christian leaders. As director of the Acts in Africa Initiative (AIA), I have sat with the elected leaders of Assemblies of God national churches across Africa as they developed strategies for greater church planting and missions involvement. I have marveled at their singleness of purpose, deep consecration, and bold faith. They have uniformly demonstrated a willingness to risk all to advance God's kingdom in their own countries and beyond. Should Jesus tarry, the Africa Assemblies of God are poised to emerge as a formidable missions movement, marshalling thousands of committed cross-cultural emissaries from Sub-Saharan Africa to the yet-to-be-reached peoples of Africa and the world. I have written this book to help facilitate this God-ordained enterprise.

The twelve lessons contained herein were first taught in Acts 1:8 Conferences conducted throughout Africa by AIA. AIA is an auxiliary ministry of the Assemblies of God World Missions, USA (Africa Office). It has been commissioned by the Africa Assemblies of God Alliance (AAGA) to help inspire an authentic Pentecostal and missional awakening in the African church with the goal of igniting the greatest evangelistic, church planting, and missionary advance in the movement's 100-year history. At present, the Africa Assemblies of God comprise 50 national churches in Sub-Sahara Africa and the Indian Ocean Basin. The movement includes 83,000 local churches and 22 million adherents.

Since 2010, AIA has led AAGA's "Decade of Pentecost" emphasis.[1] The Decade of Pentecost is a continent-wide missions initiative beginning on Pentecost Sunday, 2010, and extending through Pentecost Sunday, 2020. The principal aim of the program is

---

[1] Website: www.DecadeofPentecost.org

to see 10 million new believers baptized in the Holy Spirit and mobilized as Spirit-empowered witnesses at home and to the ends of the earth. True to its aim, this powerful missional emphasis has helped to inspire AG churches across Africa to plant thousands of new churches, lead millions of people to faith in Christ, and deploy hundreds of new indigenous African missionaries to the yet-to-be-reached tribes of Sub-Sahara Africa and beyond.

As mentioned above, one way AIA has served AAGA is by developing and conducting Acts 1:8 Conferences across the continent. These missions mobilization conferences are designed to help AG national churches prepare themselves for greater Spirit-empowered evangelism, church planting, and missions. A typical conference lasts from 4-6 days and is structured around a twelve lesson core curriculum, expounding, explaining, and applying the dual emphasis of Jesus' final promise to the church found in Acts 1:8: *"You will receive power...and you will be my witnesses..."*[2] These lessons make up the twelve chapters of this book. They can be logically grouped as follows:

- Lessons 1-3:   Theological and philosophical foundations for Spirit-empowered mission
- Lessons 4-8:   Practical implementation of Spirit-empowered mission
- Lessons 9-12   Some important groups to involve in Spirit-empowered mission.

Each conference includes four essential components: intercessory prayer, missional instruction, strategy development, and spiritual encounter. By design, each of these components reflects the twofold emphasis of Acts 1:8, empowerment and mission. For instance, when

---

[2] In other works, I have referred to this recurring emphasis in Acts as Luke's "empowerment-witness motif," most notably in my book, *Empowered for Global Mission: A Missionary Look at the Book of Acts* (Springfield, MO: Life Publishers) 2005.

Introduction

we pray, we pray for power, and we commit ourselves to witness. When we teach, every lesson speaks in some way about Jesus' promise of power and our duty to testify about Him. When we develop our missions and church planting strategies, we apply Jesus' Acts 1:8 promise. And when we preach, we call on the people to come to be baptized in the Holy Spirit and empowered as Christ's witnesses to the lost. We do this because we are convinced that the book of Acts presents a divinely inspired missions strategy. It contains God's plan for reaching the nations for Christ before His return.

How to Use This Book

Allow me to suggest three ways you may profitably use this book. First, you can read it as you would any work on practical theology, as a means of personal growth and ministerial development. At the end of each lesson is an exercise designed to help you review and apply the lesson to yourself and to your ministerial context. These exercises have three components: reflection, application, and implementation. Using the *reflection* component, you will reflect on some important concepts found in the lesson. This will help you to assimilate the truths you have just explored. Using the *application* component, you will begin to apply the insights you have gained to your own ministerial context. Finally, using the *implementation* component, you will take some essential first steps in actually putting into practice the things you have learned. I encourage you to utilize these exercises.

A second way you may to use this book is as a tool to mobilize your church or organization for greater evangelism, church planting, and missions. You could select particular lessons in the book as a basis for creating a sermon series on Spirit-empowered Mission. This sermon series could serve as part of a broader missions mobilization strategy.

A final way you could use this book is as a guide to plan and conduct your own full-blown Acts 1:8 Conference. You could do this

Introduction

alone or as a cooperative effort with other pastors and churches in your area. The five appendices at the end of this book are designed to help you in this endeavor. Begin with "Appendix 1: Acts 1:8 Conference Planning Guide." This guide addresses many of the issues involved in creating a conference. The main issue in planning a conference is that we remain focused on the central purpose of any Acts 1:8 Conference, that is, to mobilize the church for Spirit-empowered witness, church planting, and missions.

~ Chapter 1 ~

THE HOLY SPIRIT AND THE MISSION OF GOD

In the opening chapter of Acts, Luke tells of Jesus' final hours on earth. He had already written about the Savior's suffering and death in his gospel. There, he described how Jesus was arrested, falsely charged, and publically executed. He further told of how, three days later, Jesus rose from the grave. The risen Lord then spent forty days preparing His disciples for their God-ordained mission. Five times during that period Jesus issued His "Great Commission." He ordered His followers, "Go into all the world and proclaim the gospel to the whole creation."[1] He further told them to "make disciples of all nations."[2] Finally, just before He ascended back into heaven, Jesus

---

[1] Mark 16:15
[2] Matthew 28:19. The Great Commission is also found in Luke 24:46; John 20:21; Acts 1:8.

left His church with a final command and a final promise. His command was,

> "[Do] not depart from Jerusalem, but…wait for the promise of the Father, which, he said, 'you heard from me; for John baptized with water, but you will be baptized with the Holy Spirit not many days from now.'"[3]

His promise was,

> "But you will receive power when the Holy Spirit has come upon you, and you will be my witnesses in Jerusalem and in all Judea and Samaria, and to the end of the earth."[4]

In doing this, Jesus "married" God's mission to God's empowering Presence. He was in effect saying, "I command you to go into all the world and tell people the good news concerning my saving work on the cross and my victorious resurrection from the dead. However, you are not to attempt this great work until you have first been empowered by the Holy Spirit." Or, in the words of the famous television ad, Jesus was ordering them, "Don't leave home without it!"

In this lesson, we will examine the critical relationship between God's mission and God's Spirit. In doing this, we will answer two important questions: "What is the mission of God?" and "What is the role of the Holy Spirit in fulfilling that mission?"

The Mission of God

What then do we mean by the term "mission of God?" The mission of God—sometimes referred to as the *missio Dei*—is God's purpose and work in the world in relation to fallen humanity. God's mission is to redeem and call to himself a people out of every tribe, tongue, and nation on earth. Jesus explained that this mission includes

---

[3] Acts 1:4-5
[4] Acts 1:8

every place and every people. He declared, "This gospel of the kingdom will be proclaimed throughout the whole world as a testimony to all nations, and then the end will come."[5] When this occurs, the mission of God will have been completed. In the book of Revelation, John looked into heaven and saw that day. He wrote, "After this I looked, and behold, a great multitude that no one could number, from every nation, from all tribes and peoples and languages, standing before the throne and before the Lamb..."[6]

The Bible further teaches that God's mission is moving toward a definite climax. Again, John peered into the future and saw a time when "the kingdoms of this world are become the kingdoms of our Lord, and of his Christ; and he shall reign for ever and ever."[7] Concerning that time, Paul noted, "Then comes the end, when he [Jesus] delivers the kingdom to God the Father after destroying every rule and every authority and power."[8]

From the beginning, God intended to redeem people from all nations.[9] Because He created Adam and Eve (and thus all humankind) in His own image,[10] He has a loving interest in every person. God assured Israel, "I have loved you with an everlasting love."[11] That same love extends to all people of all nations. Jesus declared that "God so loved the world..."[12] God's ultimate expression of love for humanity was demonstrated in His willingness to send His Son to die on the cross for their sins.[13]

---

[5] Matthew 24:14
[6] Revelation 7:9
[7] Revelation 11:15
[8] 1 Corinthians 15:24
[9] Jesus was "the Lamb that was slain from the creation of the world" (Revelation 13:8, NIV).
[10] Genesis 1:27
[11] Jeremiah 31:3
[12] John 3:16
[13] Romans 5:6-8

When, in the Garden of Eden, Adam yielded to temptation and sinned, all of creation fell with him.[14] Since that time, everyone who has ever lived has participated in Adam's rebellion. The Bible tells us, "All have sinned and fall short of the glory of God."[15] Because of this, everyone needs a Savior. Jesus came to make a way for everyone everywhere to be reconciled to God.

Centuries before Jesus came, God promised to send a Savior to redeem fallen humanity. When He called Abraham, He told him, "In you all the families of the earth shall be blessed."[16] God later revealed to Abraham, "In your offspring ["seed" KJV] shall all the nations of the earth be blessed."[17] Paul explained that Jesus was that "seed."[18] He is truly "the Savior of the world."[19] The entire Bible reveals and enlarges on God's plan to redeem the nations. As God's missionary people, we have been called to join Him in this mission.[20]

The Missionary Nature of God

God's mission flows from His nature. He is by nature a missionary God. When we think of missions, we often think of the Great Commission, as mentioned above. This is good. We should often remind ourselves of this command of Christ. However, as important as this is, our understanding of God's mission must go deeper. We must understand that God's very essence is missional. It is in His nature to reach out in love to those He created. Because God is a missionary God,

---

[14] Genesis 3:6; Romans 5:12
[15] Romans 3:23
[16] Genesis 12:3
[17] Genesis 22:18
[18] Galatian 3:16
[19] 1 John 4:14
[20] John 20:21-22

- He created humankind in His own image.[21]
- He inspired the Bible to make himself known to those He created.[22]
- He raised up Israel and called them to be a light to the nations.[23]
- He sent His Son, Jesus, to die on the cross for the sins of all people everywhere.[24]
- He sends His church into the world to preach the good news to all nations.[25]
- He sends His Spirit to empower His church to witness to all people before Christ returns.[26]

Think about it, missions does not exist because Christ commissioned the church. Rather, Christ commissioned the church because God has a mission. The church therefore owes its very existence to the mission of God. The Swiss theologian, Emil Brunner, famously stated, "As fire exists by burning, the church exists by mission." To put it another way, where there is no burning, there is no fire. In the same way, where there is no mission, there is no church.

Jesus came to fulfill God's mission. He made the way for all people everywhere to be saved. He now commissions us, His missionary people, to continue His redemptive mission. What He said to His first disciples, He says to us today, "As the Father has sent me, even so I am sending you"[27]

---

[21] Genesis 1:26-27
[22] 2 Timothy 3:16; 2 Peter 1:20-21
[23] Isaiah 42:6
[24] John 3:16; 2 Corinthians 5:15; 1 John 4:14
[25] John 20:22
[26] Luke 24:46-49; Acts 1:8
[27] John 20:21

God's Missionary Spirit

Because God is a missionary God, the Holy Spirit—who is himself God—is a missionary Spirit. He is that member of the Holy Trinity who, in this age, carries out God's mission in the earth. This fact is seen many places in Scripture. For instance, it is seen in the ministry of Jesus. Quoting Isaiah, Jesus said of himself,

> "The Spirit of the Lord is upon me, because he has anointed me to proclaim good news to the poor. He has sent me to proclaim liberty to the captives and recovering of sight to the blind, to set at liberty those who are oppressed, to proclaim the year of the Lord's favor."[28]

Jesus was saying that the Spirit of the Lord had anointed and enabled Him to fulfill His God-given mission. Peter further described how "God anointed Jesus of Nazareth with the Holy Spirit and with power. He went about doing good and healing all who were oppressed by the devil, for God was with him."[29]

The Spirit's role in missions is possibly most clearly stated in Jesus' final promise to the church: "But you will receive power when the Holy Spirit has come upon you, and you will be my witnesses in Jerusalem and in all Judea and Samaria, and to the end of the earth."[30] (This is the guiding verse of our study, so get ready to hear it repeated again and again.) In this declaration, Jesus left the church with two clear directives: First, we are to be His witnesses at home and to the remotest parts of the earth. But before we do this, we are to wait until the Spirit comes on us to empower us for the work.

Jesus' words in Acts 1:8 thus established a pattern followed throughout the book of Acts. Without exception, every outpouring of the Holy Spirit in Acts results in powerful missional witness. Put another way, every forward movement of the church in Acts is

---

[28] Luke 4:17-18; cf. Isaiah 61:1-2
[29] Acts 10:38
[30] Acts 1:8

preceded by one or more outpourings of the Holy Spirit. From this insight, we learn a powerful lesson. If we, as God's missionary people, are to effectively participate in His mission to redeem the nations, we, like Jesus and the apostles, must be empowered by the Spirit.

Our Missionary Responsibility

What then is our missionary responsibility concerning the Holy Spirit? It is fourfold:

First, we must commit ourselves wholeheartedly to Christ and His redemptive mission. Christ once challenged Peter and Andrew, "Follow me, and I will make you fishers of men."[31] The two brothers immediately left their fishing business and joined Jesus in His mission. Peter would later confess to Jesus, "We have left all and followed thee."[32] We must do the same, remembering that God promises to give His Spirit to those who obey Him.[33]

Next, we must acquire a clear understanding of the missional purpose of the baptism in the Holy Spirit. The Bible clearly teaches that, at its core, the baptism in the Holy Spirit is a missionally empowering experience. We must allow this essential truth to pervade our very being. We must further understand that, when we preach on the baptism in the Holy Spirit, and pray with others to be filled with the Spirit, we are mobilizing them for mission. This is what Jesus was doing when He commanded His disciples to "stay in the city until you are clothed with power from on high."[34] By leading our people into the baptism in the Holy Spirit, we are helping to prepare them to effectively participate in the *missio Dei*.

---

[31] Mark 4:19
[32] Luke 18:28 (KJV).
[33] Acts 5:32; cf. vv. 28-29
[34] Luke 24:49

Third, we must ourselves personally experience the Spirit's empowering, as did Jesus and the early disciples.[35] Before we can lead others into Spirit-empowered evangelism, church planting, and missions, we must ensure that we ourselves have been empowered by the Spirit—and that we are currently walking and ministering in the Spirit's power. Jesus once told His disciples, "Everyone who is fully trained will be like their teacher."[36] If we will lead others into Spirit-empowered ministry, we ourselves must first become Spirit-empowered ministers. Only then can we say with Paul, "Follow my example, as I follow the example of Christ."[37]

Finally, in response to what we have learned in this lesson, we must wholeheartedly commit ourselves to preach and teach often and effectively on the baptism in the Holy Spirit. Our people must understand the absolute necessity of their being empowered by the Spirit to fully participate in God's mission. We must further provide many opportunities for our people to be filled and refilled with the Spirit. All along, we must show them what it looks like to live and minister in the Spirit's power. The lessons that follow in this book will help prepare us for this task.

Review and Application

Now that you have completed this lesson, take a few moments to reflect, apply, and implement the things you have learned.

Reflect:

Reflect on the following issues:

- Explain what is meant by the term "mission of God."
- When we say that "God is a missionary God," what do we mean?

---

[35] Luke 3:21-22, cf. 4:18-19; Acts 2
[36] Luke 6:40 (NIV)
[37] 1 Corinthians 11:1 (NIV)

- Describe the role of the Spirit in fulfilling God's mission in the earth.
- Explain the meaning of the saying, "As fire exists by burning, the Church exists by mission."

Apply:

Now, make the following applications to your present ministry:

- If God is a missionary God, what does that say about us as His people?
- Think about your church. How does it measure up to this saying?

Commit:

Finally, pray this prayer and make this commitment:

- *Prayer:* "Oh Holy Spirit, I yield myself to you. Come and empower me as you empowered the early Christians in the book of Acts."
- *Commitment:* "I commit myself to Christ and His mission. In doing this, I will be filled with, and seek to remain full of, the Holy Spirit. And, I will lead others into the Spirit-empowered life."

Notes:

~ Chapter 2 ~

SPIRIT BAPTISM REVISITED[1]

In Chapter 1, we discussed the concept of the *missio Dei,* or the mission of God. We defined God's mission as His purpose and work in the world in relation to fallen humanity, and we discovered that the Creator God is on a mission to redeem and call unto himself a people out of every tribe, tongue, and nation on earth. We further examined the essential role of the Holy Spirit in fulfilling that mission. We learned that, without the Spirit's presence and power in our lives, we would never be able to accomplish the work.

In this lesson, we will discuss God's chosen means of transferring His divine power to His missionary people. He does this through a powerful spiritual experience known as the baptism in the Holy Spirit. John the Baptist, Jesus, and Peter all spoke of this experience.[2] Just before He ascended back into heaven, Jesus promised His disciples, "You will be baptized with the Holy Spirit not many days from

---

[1] This lesson was originally developed by AIA team member, Mark R. Turney. Most of what is said here reflect his thoughts on the subject.

[2] Luke 3:16; Acts 1:5; Acts 11:16

now."[3] About a week later, on the Day of Pentecost, He first fulfilled the promise by pouring out His Spirit on 120 waiting disciples. The Bible describes their experience like this:

> "When the day of Pentecost arrived, they were all together in one place. And suddenly there came from heaven a sound like a mighty rushing wind, and it filled the entire house where they were sitting. And divided tongues as of fire appeared to them and rested on each one of them. And they were all filled with the Holy Spirit and began to speak in other tongues as the Spirit gave them utterance."[4]

This Pentecostal experience became the normal experience and ongoing practice of the New Testament church. Throughout Acts, we read of believers being baptized in—and thus empowered by—the Holy Spirit.[5] In this lesson, we will consider four issues concerning this powerful spiritual experience as it relates to the missionary practice of the church today. First, we will discuss the *purpose* of Spirit baptism. Then, we will examine the tragic *neglect* of the experience in today's church. Next, we will consider our need to *remedy* this shortcoming. And finally, we will recommend a *plan* to help us refocus on the experience.

The Purpose of Spirit Baptism

Before returning to heaven, Jesus ordered His disciples to wait in Jerusalem for the coming of the Holy Spirit. He explained to them why their obedience was so important. He said, "You will receive power when the Holy Spirit has come upon you, and you will be my witnesses in Jerusalem and in all Judea and Samaria, and to the end of

---

[3] Acts 1:5

[4] Acts 2:1-4; cf. v. 33

[5] Acts 8:16-17; 9:17-18; 10:44-47; 19:6. In Acts, Luke uses several images to describe Spirit baptism, including being "baptized in" the Holy Spirit, being "filled with" the Spirit, the Spirit "coming on" individuals, and others.

the earth."[6] He knew that they would need to be baptized in the Holy Spirit for they would need God's power to accomplish God's work—the evangelization of the nations. In a parallel passage, Jesus described Spirit baptism as a "clothing with power from on high."[7] He explained that this heavenly clothing would enable His followers to effectually proclaim repentance for the forgiveness of sins to all nations.[8]

Thus, the primary purpose of Spirit baptism is to supply the power needed to fulfill the mission of God. Someone once asked an old Pentecostal preacher, "Sir, why do you so strongly insist that every Christian be baptized in the Holy Spirit?" The preacher did not hesitate. "Every Christian must be baptized in the Holy Spirit," he replied, "because every Christian is called to be Christ's witness." It is through Spirit baptism that God enables us to effectively witness for Christ.

As mentioned in Chapter 1, this fact is demonstrated throughout the book of Acts. As the story progresses, God pours out His Spirit again and again. Without exception, every outpouring of the Spirit is followed by a mighty surge of Spirit-anointed witness.[9] For instance, in Acts 4:31 the Bible says, "And when they had prayed, the place in which they were gathered together was shaken, and they were all filled with the Holy Spirit and continued to speak the word of God with boldness." The empowering of the Holy Spirit thus enabled the early disciples to effectively proclaim the gospel to the lost. It also enabled them to perform confirmatory signs and wonders in the name of the risen Jesus.[10]

---

[6] Acts 1:8
[7] Luke 24:49
[8] Luke 24:47
[9] Acts 2:4-41; 4:8-12; 4:31-33; 6:10; 8:15-17 w/ 9:31; 9:17-20; 10:44-46 with 11:15; 19:6-10
[10] Acts 3:1-10; 5:12-16; 6:8; 8:4-8; 9:32-35, 40; 13:9-12; 14:8-10; 15:12

By telling these stories, Luke shows his readers the dynamic effect of Spirit baptism on the lives of Christians. He demonstrates what one can expect to happen when he or she fully commit themselves to God's mission and are then empowered by the Spirit.

This empowering experience is available to every believer. Peter declared, "The promise is for you and for your children and for all who are far off, everyone whom the Lord our God calls to himself."[11]

The Neglect of Spirit Baptism

In light of these enormous benefits, it would seem that every Pentecostal pastor and leader would often stress the importance of Spirit baptism in his or her teaching and preaching. Statistics, however, tell a different story. They indicate a waning emphasis on Spirit baptism in many Classical Pentecostal churches. As a result, fewer and fewer people attending these churches are being filled with the Spirit. In many such settings, members have even begun to doubt the necessity of the experience or its present day validity.

These twin maladies of experiential and theological drift have plunged many formerly spiritually alive churches into a downward spiral toward nominalism. In other words, while remaining Pentecostal in name, these churches are no longer Pentecostal in experience and practice. While this downturn in authentic Pentecostal experience has been mitigated in the Africa Assemblies of God during their Decade of Pentecost emphasis from 2010 to 2020,[12] much remains to be done.

This neglect of Spirit baptism in Pentecostal churches poses a serious threat to the missionary advance of the church. Since the purpose of Spirit baptism is to empower God's people to fulfill the Great Commission, and since only a minority of those attending

---

[11] Acts 2:38-39

[12] Website: www.DecadeofPentecost.org

Pentecostal churches have been baptized in the Holy Spirit, the question arises, "If we fail to emphasize this experience, how will we ever be able to fulfill Christ's mandate to be His witnesses at home and to the ends of the earth?"

A number of factors could be driving this alarming trend. One is the misguided emphasis of many Pentecostal churches on personal blessing and material prosperity rather than commitment to God and His mission. Another contributing factor is the pressure that some Pentecostal leaders feel to accommodate non-Pentecostal and mainstream churches in their locales. In addition, there is the natural inclination in the heart of every Christian to depend on human effort rather than the power of the Spirit.

When tempted to move away from their historic emphasis on Spirit baptism, Pentecostal leaders would do well to remember the admonition of Paul to the churches in Galatia. "O foolish Galatians!" he challenged, "who has bewitched you? Are you so foolish? Having begun by the Spirit, are you now being perfected by the flesh?"[13] To ignore the gift of the Holy Spirit is to ignore God's chosen means of reaching the nations with the gospel. We must never make this grave mistake.

The Need of the Hour

No Pentecostal church can remain authentically Pentecostal without regular outpourings of the Spirit. While other non-Pentecostal churches can remain true to their historic roots without such outpourings, this cannot be said of a Pentecostal church. For it to remain truly Pentecostal, its members must be repeatedly filled with the Spirit according to the biblical command to "keep being filled with the Holy Spirit."[14]

---

[13] Galatians 3:1, 3
[14] Literal translation of Ephesians 5:18

Further, if the African church is to effectively engage in God's mission, and fulfill its missionary destiny to reach all of Africa and the nations for Christ, it must experience a powerful continent-wide outpouring of the Spirit. For this to happen, pastors must preach regularly and effectively on the baptism in the Holy Spirit. They must then pray with their members to be filled with the Spirit. Finally, according to the pattern established in Acts, pastors must mobilize their churches and lead them into Spirit-empowered witness, church planting, and missions.[15]

A Way Forward

The question arises, what can a pastor or church leader do to ensure that their members are empowered by the Holy Spirit and effectively engaged in reaching the lost with the gospel? Here are five practical strategies they can employ to achieve these ends:

1. Become convinced. Before a pastor can lead his or her members into Spirit-empowered ministry, they must first recognize the need. They must be persuaded that their people really need to be empowered by the Holy Spirit. If the pastor is not convinced, little else will follow. The church will remain powerless, infertile, and largely ineffective. One way leaders can become convinced of the need for the Spirit's power is to study the ministries of Jesus and the apostles. They will discover how passionate both were in ensuring that their disciples were filled with the Holy Spirit.

Jesus demanded that His disciples remain in Jerusalem to be empowered by the Spirit before going to the lost to proclaim the good news.[16] Following His example, the apostles and early church leaders

---

[15] This is what Paul did in Acts 19:1-10
[16] Luke 24:49; Act 1:4-5

insisted that new converts be immediately empowered by the Spirit.[17] We must do the same in our churches today.

2. Be filled. Next, if Pentecostal leaders are to see their people baptized in the Spirit and empowered as Christ's witnesses to the lost, they themselves must be personally filled with the Spirit, as we have already stated. They must further learn to live and minister in the Spirit's power. For how can they lead their people into an experience they do not themselves possess? Pastors and other church leaders must therefore commit themselves to maintaining the fullness of the Spirit in their own lives and ministries.

3. Pray. Next, the Pentecostal pastor must devote himself or herself to ongoing prayer that God would pour out His Spirit on the church. They must further ask God to instill growing vision for witness and missions in the hearts of the people. The pastor will want to invite his or her committed laypeople to join them in ongoing prayer for true Pentecostal revival.

4. Preach and teach. If a pastor is serious about seeing his or her members empowered by the Spirit, they will preach and teach often on the need for every disciple to be baptized in the Holy Spirit. In doing this, they will highlight the relationship between the Holy Spirit and missions. For example, a pastor could preach a series of sermons focusing on outpourings of the Spirit in the book of Acts. As he does this, he should note how each of those outpourings resulted in powerful Spirit-anointed witness.[18] After each message, he should call

---

[17] Acts 8:14-17; 9:17-18; 19:1-7

[18] The Acts in Africa Initiative has produced three sermon outline books that can help: (1) *Proclaiming Pentecost: 100 Sermon Outlines on the Power of the Holy Spirit;* (2) *Proclaiming Christ to the Nations: 100 Sermon Outlines on Spirit-Empowered Mission;* and (3) *Interceding for the Nations: 100 Sermon Outlines on Missional Prayer.* These books can be purchased from the Acts in Africa Initiative in paperback format or downloaded free in e-book format (PDF) at www.DecadeofPentecost.org.

the people to prayer, giving them an opportunity to be filled and refilled with the Holy Spirit.

5. Mobilize. Finally, once his or her members have been baptized in the Spirit, and have committed themselves to God's mission, the wise Pentecostal pastor will begin to mobilize them for Spirit-empowered witness. To fail to do this will diminish the empowering work of the Spirit in the people's lives. However, if we will do these things, we will see our churches grow and multiply. We will see God's mission advance in Africa and to the ends of the earth.

Review and Application

Now that you have completed this lesson, take a few moments to reflect, apply, and implement the things you have learned.

Reflect:

Reflect on the following issues:

- According to Scripture, what is the primary purpose of the baptism in the Holy Spirit?
- Discuss the tragic results of failing to teach and preach on the baptism in the Holy Spirit.

Apply:

Now, make the following applications to your present ministry:

- Conduct a mental review of your recent ministry by asking the following questions: How often do I preach and teach on the baptism in the Holy Spirit? When I do preach on the topic, do I emphasize the need to be empowered for mission?
- Now, list some adjustments you can make to better emphasize Spirit baptism in your ministry context.

Commit:

Finally, pray this prayer and make this commitment:

- *Prayer:* "Spirit of God, anoint me and help me to lead my members into the baptism in the Holy Spirit. Then, enable me to mobilize them for Spirit-empowered witness."
- *Commitment:* "Heavenly Father, I commit to doing what is necessary in my own experience and in my church to see my people baptized in the Holy Spirit and empowered as Christ's witnesses. I will strive to live the Spirit-empowered life, and I will teach my people to do the same. I will lead them into Spirit-empowered witness and church planting."

Notes:

~ Chapter 3 ~

WHAT IT MEANS TO BE PENTECOSTAL

What is your vision of Pentecostalism? If someone were to ask you, "In your opinion, what makes one a true Pentecostal?" or "What qualities lie at the heart of one's being a Pentecostal Christian?" How would you respond? If you are like most people attending Pentecostal churches today, you would have difficulty with your answer.

In this lesson, we will address this important issue. We will do this by first looking at the widespread confusion among Pentecostals concerning who they are and what God intends them be. We will then suggest four core characteristics of authentic Pentecostalism.

Confusion in Pentecostalism

In its just over 100 years of existence, modern Pentecostalism has grown into a worldwide movement. Researchers estimate that there are more than one million "renewalist" churches scattered across the globe today.[1] The movement continues to expand at an astonishing rate. Nowhere is this expansion more evident than in Africa.

While this impressive growth has many positive aspects, it has also given birth to some significant challenges. With growth has come diversity, and with diversity confusion. In the world today, there exist literally hundreds of versions of Pentecostalism. In an effort to better understand this great diversity, scholars have attempted to divide Pentecostalism into more manageable subgroupings. For instance, some have grouped them as Classical Pentecostals, Charismatics (or Neo-Pentecostals), and Third Wavers (or Neo-Charismatics).[2] Others have grouped them in other ways. Each subgrouping is then divided into even smaller sub-subgroups—and so it goes. In Africa, this "Pentecostal mishmash" is complicated even further with the addition of the various Pentecostal-like AIC's across the continent.[3] The point is, in modern Pentecostalism there exists a near mindboggling diversity.

This diversity has contributed to widespread uncertainty among even Classical Pentecostals. Adherents are no longer certain of what it means to be authentically Pentecostal. This uncertainty has found its

---

[1] "Renewalist" is a term used by some scholars to describe churches that emphasize the work of the Holy Spirit, spiritual gifts, and modern-day miracles as an everyday part of a believer's life.

[2] The Classical Pentecostals are identified as those churches who trace their origin to the Azusa Street Outpouring of 1906-1908. They form such denominations as the Assemblies of God, the Church of God (Cleveland, Tennessee), the Foursquare Gospel Church, and others. The Charismatics are those churches that trace their origins back to the outpourings of the Spirit on the historic denominations beginning in the 1960s. The Third Wavers are those who trace their origins to the move of the Spirit among the traditional Evangelical churches in the 1980s.

[3] Variously called African Indigenous Churches, African Initiated Churches, or African Independent Churches.

way into the Africa Assemblies of God.[4] Many African pastors and church members have been so affected by the religious winds swirling across the continent that they suffer from "identity crises." They have no clear idea of who they are as Pentecostals, or why God has called them into His kingdom.

If Assemblies of God (and other) pastors and church members are to fulfill their God-ordained mission in the earth, they must "find themselves." In other words, they must come to a clear understanding of what it means to be authentically Pentecostal. If this issue is not dealt with swiftly and decisively, it could stall the missionary advance of the church.

An Authoritative Model

Where then shall we look for an authoritative model of authentic Pentecostalism? Shall we mindlessly mimic what we see happening in "successful" ministries and churches we view on our television screens? Or shall we imitate what we have observed in the "megachurch" in the nearby city? How foolish we would be to do such things. Rather, as "people of the Book," we must look to inspired Scripture for our answers. More specifically, we must look into the New Testament book of Acts as a model for our churches today. For Acts is the only divinely inspired account we have of how the early church actually carried out its mission.

As Pentecostals, we believe Acts to be more than a book of history. We believe it presents a divinely inspired model of what the church ought to be and how it ought to function until Jesus comes again. While others may view Acts as a mere historical record of what happened in the church *then and there,* Pentecostals view it as a

---

[4] By "Africa Assemblies of God," we refer to the fifty national churches comprising about 83,000 local churches associated with the Africa Assemblies of God Alliance (AAGA). The same confusion likely holds true for Assemblies of God churches around the world.

manual for life and ministry describing what the church should look like *here and now.* We believe it to be an enduring model of how the church must publish the good news of Christ until the end of the age.

Biblically defined, authentic Pentecostalism is *a popular, last-days, Spirit-empowered missionary movement.* Let's unpack this definition.

- When we say that true Pentecostalism is a *movement,* we mean that it is more than a church or denomination. It is a Spirit-driven movement of people passionately pursuing a common cause.
- When we say that it is a *missionary* movement, we mean that its *raison d'etre* (reason for being) is to fulfill Christ's command to make disciples of all nations.
- When we say that authentic Pentecostalism is a *Spirit-empowered* missionary movement, we mean that it seeks to carry out its mission in the power of the Holy Spirit as mandated by Jesus in Acts 1:8.
- When we say that it is a *last-days* Spirit-empowered missionary movement, we mean that Pentecostals believe that Jesus could come at any moment. This understanding instills in them a sense of urgency to complete the mission.
- When we say that true Pentecostalism is a *popular* last-days Spirit-empowered missionary movement, we mean it belongs to the people. Pentecostalism is the "great democratizer," for true Pentecostals believe that through the empowerment of the Spirit any Christian, no matter how poor or marginalized, can fully and effectively participate in God's mission.

Further, to be truly Pentecostal means four essential things. It means that one preaches the *same message,* shares the *same mission,* embraces the *same experiences,* and employs the *same methods* as did the church in the book of Acts. Let's look at each of these four principal characteristics of authentic Pentecostalism.

Same Message

To be truly Pentecostal means that *we proclaim the same message as did the church in the book of Acts*. That message is the gospel of Jesus Christ. It is the story of how Jesus died on the cross for the sins of humanity, and how He rose victoriously from the grave on the third day.[5] True proclamation of the gospel further involves calling people to repentance and faith in Christ.[6] Pentecostals understand that the gospel is the only message that can lead people to eternal life.[7] Because of this, the true Pentecostal is committed to faithfully proclaiming Christ to all.[8]

The gospel message is at the heart of all preaching in the book of Acts. For instance, Luke tells how Philip "went down to the city of Samaria and began proclaiming Christ to them."[9] Later, when Philip encountered an Ethiopian nobleman, he "told him the good news about Jesus."[10] On another occasion, when the Roman jailer asked Paul, "What must I do to be saved?" the apostle did not hesitate. "Believe in the Lord Jesus," he replied, "and you will be saved."[11] The true Pentecostal will do the same. He or she will faithfully proclaim the gospel of Christ to all who will listen.

A close examination of the sermons preached in Acts reveals that the apostles and other preachers consistently addressed certain key themes.[12] Biblical scholars have labeled these themes as the

---

[5] 1 Corinthians 15:1-3
[6] Acts 20:21-22; cf. Mark 1:15
[7] John 6:68; 14:6; Acts 4:12
[8] Romans 15:19-20; 1 Corinthians 1:23
[9] Acts 8:5 (NASB)
[10] Acts 8:35
[11] Acts 16:31
[12] Those sermons include Peter at Pentecost, 2:14-40; Peter again (3:12-26); Peter and John (4:5-12); Stephen (7:1-53); Peter again (10:28-47); Paul (13:16-21; 14:3-4; 17:22-35).

"apostolic kerygma." *Kerygma* is the Greek word used in the New Testament meaning "proclamation." These key themes include the following:

- Jesus is the promised Messiah, the fulfillment of Old Testament prophecies.[13]
- Jesus died on the cross for the sins of humankind.[14]
- Jesus rose triumphantly from the grave proving that He is indeed the Christ.[15]
- Jesus ascended into heaven and pours out the Holy Spirit as is promised in Scripture.[16]
- Jesus will come again to judge all people.[17]
- To be reconciled to God, all must repent of their sins and put their faith in Christ alone for salvation.[18]

As did the apostles in Acts, the authentic Pentecostal will focus his or her preaching and teaching on these same key biblical themes.

Early Pentecostal preaching centered on what they called the "full gospel." This full gospel contained four major themes: Jesus saves, Jesus heals, Jesus baptizes in the Holy Spirit, and Jesus is coming again. This fourfold emphasis helped keep early Pentecostals focused on the essentials of the gospel. Today, however, many nominal Pentecostals have abandoned these key themes. Sadly, some are even compromising the gospel. They are focusing on such themes a personal blessing and material prosperity. Consequently, many people in their churches remain in their sins unprepared for eternity. These

---

[13] Acts 2:25-36
[14] Acts 2:22-23
[15] Acts 2:24-32; 4:10-11
[16] Acts 2:33
[17] Acts 10:42; 17:31
[18] Acts 2:38-39; 4:12

pseudo-Pentecostal preachers should listen well to Paul's admonition to the Galatians:

> "I am astonished that you are so quickly deserting him who called you in the grace of Christ and are turning to a different gospel—not that there is another one, but there are some who trouble you and want to distort the gospel of Christ. But even if we or an angel from heaven should preach to you a gospel contrary to the one we preached to you, let him be accursed."[19]

To be authentically Pentecostal means that we faithfully and consistently proclaim the same message as the church in Acts—the gospel of Jesus Christ.

Same Mission

Second, to be truly Pentecostal means that *we engage the same mission as did the church in the book of Acts.* Jesus clearly defined that mission in Acts 1:8: "But you will receive power when the Holy Spirit has come upon you, and you will be my witnesses in Jerusalem and in all Judea and Samaria, and to the end of the earth."

These words of Jesus represent His final declaration of the Great Commission before He returned to heaven. During the forty days between His resurrection and ascension, Jesus often taught about the kingdom of God.[20] As stated in Chapter 1, His primary kingdom theme during that time was the Great Commission, which He restated at least five times.[21] He wanted to implant this all-important concept deep into the hearts of His disciples. We must allow the Spirit to do the same in our hearts today.

---

[19] Galatians 1:6-8

[20] Acts 1:3

[21] Matthew 28:18-20; Mark 16:15-18; Luke 24:46-49; John 20:21-22; Acts 1:8

Early Pentecostals were committed to fulfilling Christ's commission in the power of the Holy Spirit. Three deeply held beliefs drove them to the ends of the earth to proclaim the good news. First, they truly believed that Jesus' coming was imminent and that He could come at any moment. Next, they believed that Christ had commissioned the church to proclaim the gospel to all nations before He returned. And finally, they believed that in these last days of time, God was pouring out His Spirit as the promised "latter rain" spoken of by the prophets.[22] This promised outpouring was for the express purpose of empowering the church to complete the Great Commission before Christ returned.

Pentecostals further believed that this divine power could be personally appropriated through a biblical experience known as the baptism in the Holy Spirit. The melding of these deep-rooted convictions energized early Pentecostals, driving them to the ends of the earth to proclaim the good news of eternal life in Christ. If we seek to be truly Pentecostal today, we would do well to follow in the footsteps of these Pentecostal pioneers.

Same Experiences

Third, to be truly Pentecostal means that *we embrace the same experiences as did the believers in the book of Acts.* Someone has described Pentecostalism as a "rebellion against dead orthodoxy." Pentecostals contend that right belief is not enough. It is not enough to know about God, one must know Him personally. They must personally encounter Christ and fully commit themselves to Him and His will for their lives. The authentic Pentecostal, however, is not satisfied with just any spiritual experience. They hold only to those experiences of the saints found in Scripture. They particularly embrace the experiences of the early disciples recorded in the book of Acts. What, then, are those experiences?

---

[22] Joel 2:23; Zechariah 10:1; James 5:7

Life transformation. First, disciples in Acts experienced a powerful life-changing encounter with the resurrected Savior. They repented of their sins, put their full trust in Christ, and were saved. This experience permanently altered their lives, bringing them into a living relationship with God. This life transformation is clearly demonstrated in the conversion of Saul of Tarsus (Paul) on the Damascus road.[23] There, he encountered the resurrected Jesus and was miraculously transformed from a blasphemer of Christ into one of His greatest advocates. Years later, Paul wrote to the Galatians reminding them,

"You have heard of my former life in Judaism, how I persecuted the church of God violently and tried to destroy it....[But God] was pleased to reveal his Son to me."[24]

Jesus depicted this experience as a new birth.[25] In Acts, this new relationship with Christ resulted in a life of overflowing joy.[26]

Water baptism. Further, those who met Christ were immediately baptized in water.[27] Their baptism symbolized their new life in Christ and their submission to God and His mission. As a result, they separated themselves from the world and fully committed themselves to God and His purposes.[28] The authentic Pentecostal is one whose life has been changed by Christ. In addition, he or she expects that, when others encounter Christ, their lives will be transformed as well.

Divine intervention. Further, in Acts we read of the early Christians fully trusting God to supply their physical and spiritual

---

[23] Acts 9:1-18; cf. 22:6-16; 26:12-23. Other conversion stories in Acts include the 3,000 a Pentecost (2:27-44), the Samaritans (8:5-15), the Ethiopian nobleman (8:35-36), Cornelius' household (Acts 10:30-47), Lydia (16:13-15), and the Philippian jailer (16:26-31).

[24] Galatians 1:13, 16. See also 1 Timothy 1:12-15

[25] John 3:3, 7

[26] Acts 8:8; 13:52

[27] Acts 2:41; 8:12-13, 36-38; 9:18; 10:48; 16:15; 33, 18:8; 19:5

[28] Acts 2:42-47

needs. Some were delivered from demonic bondages.[29] Others were healed of various physical maladies.[30] This was all accomplished in Jesus' name and through the power of the Spirit.

Spirit baptism. This being said, the defining experience for Christians in the book of Acts is an empowering experience Jesus and the apostles described as a baptism in the Holy Spirit.[31] Throughout the book, those who were saved were encouraged to be immediately baptized in the Holy Spirit.[32] This experience is variously described as the "gift of the Holy Spirit," the Spirit "coming on" or "falling on" believers, believers being "baptized in" the Holy Spirit, "receiving" the Spirit, and being "filled" with the Holy Spirit.[33]

Using Acts as their guide, Pentecostals thus define Spirit-baptism as a powerful life-changing spiritual experience for all believers, separate from salvation, whose purpose is empowerment for mission. They further contend that the experience is always accompanied by the missional sign of speaking in tongues as the Spirit of God enables. This doctrinal formulation has encouraged Pentecostals to earnestly desire and avidly seek after this empowering experience. It has helped to catapult the Pentecostal church around the world.

---

[29] Some examples are the people of Samaria (8:7), the slave girl in Philippi (16:16-18), and the people of Ephesus (19:11-12).

[30] Acts 3:1-11; 9:33-34, 36-41; 14:19-20; 20:9-12

[31] Luke 3:16; Acts 1:5; 11:16

[32] Including the new Samaritan believers (8:16-17); Saul of Tarsus (9:17-18); and the twelve Ephesian disciples (19:1-7)

[33] Gift (2:38; 10:45); coming on (1:8; 8:16; 10:44-45; 11:15; 19:6); baptized in (1:5; 11:16); receiving (2:38; 8:15-17; 10:47; 19:2); filled with (2:4; 4:8, 31; 9:17; 13:9. 52)

Same Methods

Finally, to be authentically Pentecostal means that *we employ the same methods used by the church in the book of Acts*. As stated above, Pentecostals believe that the book of Acts was written to provide a divinely inspired strategy for reaching the nations with the gospel before Jesus returns. It is the story of how the early church imitated and implemented the strategy used by Jesus to fulfill His mission on earth. Pentecostals believe that, if the church will faithfully employ these methods, they can expect the same success as the early church. In another work, we have termed these methods the "New Testament Strategy of the Spirit."[34]

A careful reading of the book of Acts reveals the following five missionary methods used by the apostles and other early disciples:

1. Spirit-anointed proclamation. The first missionary method employed by the church in the book of Acts is powerful Spirit-anointed proclamation of the gospel. Jesus proclaimed the good news through the power of the Holy Spirit,[35] and He charged His disciples to do the same.[36] In Acts, Luke presents several instances of such Spirit-anointed preaching.

A prime example is Peter's Pentecost discourse.[37] While we often refer to this address as a sermon, in reality, it was more than a sermon, at least as we understand the term today. It was rather a Spirit-inspired, prophetic utterance. The Holy Spirit mightily anointed Peter's words and elevated their effects far beyond his natural

---

[34] Denzil R. Miller and Mark R. Turney, *The New Testament Strategy of the Spirit: An Acts 1:8 Model for 21st Century Church Planting in Africa* (Springfield, MO: AIA Publications, 2017). Available in English and French in free e-book format (PDF) at www.DecadeofPentecost.org.

[35] Luke 4:18-19; John 6:63; Acts 10:38

[36] Luke 24:49; Acts 1:8

[37] Acts 2:14-41

abilities. As a result, his words made a powerful impression on his hearers. The Bible says they were "cut to the heart," and they cried out, "Brothers, what shall we do?"[38] In response, Peter called on them to "repent and be baptized every one of you in the name of Jesus Christ for the forgiveness of your sins…" The people responded, and about 3,000 souls were swept into the kingdom of God. Peter's Spirit-anointed sermon set the pattern for preaching throughout the entire book of Acts.[39]

2. Planting missionary churches. Not only did the apostles proclaim the gospel in the Spirit's power, they intentionally planted Spirit-empowered missionary churches. Again, they were following the example of Jesus. He proclaimed the good news, calling on the people to follow Him. Those who obeyed, He took and fashioned them into the church. He then ordered them to be empowered by the Spirit, and to go and "make disciples of all nations" just as He had done with them.[40] In Acts, we observe the apostles following the lead of Jesus. They, too, intentionally planted Spirit-empowered missionary churches. Three prime examples in Acts of this strategy being implemented are the churches in Jerusalem, Antioch, and Ephesus.[41]

True Pentecostals will strive to do the same. They will clearly and powerfully proclaim the gospel to all. Those who believe, they will form into local churches. All along, they will be very deliberate about the kind of churches they plant. They will intentionally plant Spirit-empowered missionary churches. In other words, they will purposely plant churches that understand God's mission and are committed to

---

[38] Acts 2:37-38

[39] Other sermons include, Peter again (3:12-26); Peter and John (4:8-12); Stephen (7:1-53); Peter in Caesarea (10:34-47); Paul in Antioch Pisidia (13:16-41); Paul in Iconium (14:1-3); Paul in Athens (17:22-31); and more.

[40] Acts 1:4-8; Matthew 28:19

[41] Jerusalem (Acts 2-7); Antioch (11:19-24; 13:1-4); Ephesus (19:1-10)

the same. They will further ensure that the members of the church have been baptized in the Holy Spirit and empowered as Christ's witnesses. (This topic will be discussed in more detail in the next chapter.)

3. Mobilizing believers. A third method used by the apostles in Acts was the way they quickly mobilized new churches for further Spirit-empowered evangelism, missions, and church planting. This is precisely what Paul did in Ephesus in Acts 19:1-10. There, his mobilization strategy was so effective that after just two years "all the residents of Asia heard the word of the Lord, both Jews and Greeks."[42] The apostle's strategy in Ephesus involved empowering the church, proclaiming the gospel, training workers, and sending them out to proclaim the good news and plant churches throughout the entire province.[43] Again, in doing this, Paul was following the model established by Jesus, who himself called disciples, ensured that they were empowered by the Spirit, trained them, and sent them out to preach the good news and plant other Spirit-empowered missionary churches. He calls us to do the same today.

4. Divine guidance. Next, in performing their ministries, the apostles and early disciples in Acts were guided by the Holy Spirit. The Spirit showed them where they should go and what they should do to best penetrate new areas with the gospel. He directed them in various ways—through inner promptings, dreams, visions, and angelic visitations. For example, the Spirit sent Philip to Gaza to witness to an Ethiopian man.[44] He also directed Peter to Caesarea to share the good news with Cornelius' household.[45] And He guided Paul and his missionary band into Macedonia to plant churches

---

[42] Acts 19:10

[43] We discuss this strategy in more detail in our book, *The New Testament Strategy of the Spirit: An Acts 1:8 Model for 21st Century Church Planting in Africa.* (See footnote 34.)

[44] Acts 8:26-29

[45] Acts 10:9-20

there.[46] In Acts, Luke describes several other instances of such divine guidance.[47] In each instance, these early disciples were following the example of Jesus who testified, "The Son can do nothing of his own accord, but only what he sees the Father doing."[48] It is important to note that, however the guidance came, those who received it were always pointed to the harvest. If we will be prayerful and attentive to the voice of the Spirit, we can expect the Lord to do the same for us today.

5. Signs and wonders. Finally, the apostles and early disciples expected God to confirm the proclaimed word with miraculous signs and wonders as Jesus had promised.[49] These supernatural signs further demonstrated that the kingdom of God had indeed arrived in power.[50] When the people saw these demonstrations of divine power and compassion, their hearts were open to receive the message of Christ.[51] Authentic Pentecostals seek to employ the same missionary strategies. They proclaim the same message, share the same mission, embrace the same experiences, and employ the same methods used by the church in the book of Acts.

Review and Application

Paul once challenged the Christians in Corinth, "Examine yourselves, to see whether you are in the faith." In similar manner, we who call ourselves Pentecostals must take time to honestly examine ourselves, asking, "Am I an authentic Pentecostal?" Let's now take a

---

[46] Acts 16:6-10

[47] For example, Peter and John (5:19-20); Ananias (9:10-16); Cornelius (10:3.6); Barnabas and Paul (13:1-4); Paul in Corinth (18:9-10); and Paul in Jerusalem (22:18-21)

[48] John 5:19

[49] Mark 16:15-20

[50] Matthew 12:28

[51] Acts 2:12, 37; 3:9-10; 5:12-13; 8:6; 11:18; 13:11-12; 16:27-31

few moments to reflect, apply, and implement the things we have learned.

Reflect:

Having completed this lesson, reflect on the following issues:

- What do we mean when we say that Pentecostalism is having an "identity crisis"?
- List and discuss the four characteristics of authentic (that is, biblical) Pentecostalism.

Apply:

Now, evaluate your church or ministry by answering these four questions:

- Do we faithfully proclaim the *same message* as did the church in the book of Acts?
- Do we boldly engage the *same mission* as did the church in the book of Acts?
- Do we embrace the *same experiences* as did the church in the book of Acts?
- Do we use the *same methods* as did the church in the book of Acts?

Commit:

In closing, pray this prayer and make this commitment:

- *Prayer:* "Lord, thank You for showing me what it means to be authentically Pentecostal. Where I have erred, forgive me, and help me to become the kind of Christian leader found in the book of Acts."
- *Commitment:* "I commit to become an authentic Pentecostal, the kind portrayed in the book of Acts. I will preach the same message, share the same mission, embrace the same experiences, and employ the same methods as the disciples in Acts."

Notes:

~ Chapter 4 ~

PRAYER AND PENTECOSTAL REVIVAL

In the Old Testament, godly leaders often called on God to revive His people and restore His work. The Sons of Korah prayed, "Restore us again, O God of our salvation…revive us again, that your people may rejoice in you?"[1] The prophet Habakkuk prayed in similar manner, calling on God to revive His work "in the midst of the years,"[2] that is, "in this time of our deep need."[3]

While the term *revival* is not found in the New Testament, the idea of spiritual renewal is. Peter urged the people of Jerusalem to "Repent therefore, and turn again, that your sins may be blotted out, that times of refreshing may come from the presence of the Lord."[4] The book of Acts furnishes us with a vivid picture of what true revival looks like. In this book, Luke presents revival as mighty

---

[1] Psalm 85:4, 6
[2] Habakkuk 3:2
[3] New Living Translation
[4] Acts 3:19-20

outpourings of the Holy Spirit on the people of God resulting in powerful outreach to the lost.

It is significant that every call for revival in the Old Testament is coupled with prayer, and every outpouring of the Spirit in the book of Acts is preceded by the same. In this lesson, we will examine the close relationship between prayer and true Pentecostal revival. We will further commit ourselves to pursue such revival through fervent intercessory prayer and committed witness.

Pray for an Outpouring

Devoted intercession is the spark that ignites the fires of revival. In anticipation of an outpouring of God's Spirit, we must sincerely ask Him to pour out His Spirit on the church today as He did on the church in the book of Acts.

In his inspired history of the early church, Luke appears to purposefully highlight the close relationship between prayer and the outpouring of the Spirit. For example, before the outpouring of the Spirit at Pentecost, Luke tells us that the disciples "were devoting themselves to prayer."[5] Then, after the Spirit was poured out, he tells us that they continued to "devote themselves to...prayers."[6] Thus, the outpouring of the Spirit at Pentecost was both a *cause* of, and a *result* of, determined believing prayer.

Luke continues to highlight this relationship between prayer and the coming of the Spirit throughout the book of Acts. In chapter 4, he writes, *"When they had prayed* the place in which they were gathered together was shaken, and they were all filled with the Holy Spirit and continued to speak the word of God with boldness."[7] On another occasion, he tells how the apostles in Jerusalem sent Peter and John to

---

[5] Acts 1:14; cf. Luke 24:53
[6] Acts 2:42
[7] Acts 4:31 (emphasis added)

Samaria to pray with the new believers to receive the Holy Spirit.[8] Then, in chapter 9, Luke tells us how both Saul (Paul) and Ananias were in prayer before the apostle was filled with the Spirit.[9] Finally, in chapter 10, Luke informs us that both Cornelius and Peter prayed before God poured out the Spirit in Caesarea.[10]

This connection between prayer and the Spirit is in accordance with what Jesus taught His followers. He himself was in prayer when the Spirit came upon Him at His baptism.[11] He later taught His disciples that the same would happen to them. He said that the Heavenly Father would give the Holy Spirit to those who earnestly pursue Him in prayer. He told them, "I say to you, keep asking, and it [the gift of the Holy Spirit] will be given to you; keep seeking, and you will find; keep knocking, and it will be opened to you."[12] In Acts, we discover how the disciples applied this teaching to their own lives and ministries. They regularly appropriated the Spirit's power and presence through prayer.

The Bible charges every Christian to pray, asking God to fill them with the Holy Spirit. It tells how Jesus *"ordered* them [His disciples] not to depart from Jerusalem, but to wait for the promise of the Father...for John baptized with water, but you will be baptized with the Holy Spirit not many days from now."[13] The waiting that Jesus mandated in this verse is not to be interpreted as passively sitting, hoping God will fulfill His promise. Jesus was not telling His disciples to aimlessly loiter in the market chatting with their friends. He was rather directing them to continue in faith-filled prayer until they had been "clothed with power from on high."[14] The disciples

---

[8] Acts 8:15-17
[9] Ananias (Acts 9:10-16); Saul (vv. 11).
[10] Cornelius (Acts 10:1-2); Peter (vv. 9, 30-31)
[11] Luke 3:21-22
[12] Luke 11:9 (NASB, marginal reading)
[13] Acts 1:4-5
[14] Luke 24:49

obeyed Jesus' command by "devoting themselves to prayer" and by waiting "continually in the temple blessing God."[15] If we are to experience true Pentecostal revival in our day, we must do the same.

But we must not stop there. Not only must we ourselves be filled with—and remain full of—the Holy Spirit, we must ensure that every member of our churches does the same. It is essential that each one is full of the Holy Spirit and committed to God's mission. True New Testament revival will come only when God's people persevere in prayer until many are filled with the Spirit and mobilized as Spirit-empowered witnesses. Every Pentecostal pastor must therefore teach his or her deacons, elders, and other church leaders how to pray with others to be filled with the Spirit and how to then mentor them in the Spirit-empowered life.[16]

Move Out in Mission

As God begins to pour out His Spirit on the church, and believers begin to receive the Spirit, it is crucial that the pastor and church leaders begin to mobilize them for Spirit-empowered witness. This is what Jesus did with His disciples. He first sent out the twelve, then the seventy-two to proclaim the good news and to demonstrate the power of the kingdom.[17] Ultimately, He commissioned all Christians to "go into all the world and proclaim the gospel to the whole creation."[18] Before they went, however, they were to "stay in the city until [they had been] clothed with power from on high."[19]

Paul followed this same strategy in mobilizing the disciples in Ephesus. First, he ensured that they were empowered by the Holy

---

[15] Acts 1:14; Luke 24:53

[16] This topic is discussed in detail in Chapter 8, "Praying with Believers to Receive the Holy Spirit."

[17] Luke 9:1ff; Luke 10:1ff

[18] Mark 16:15

[19] Luke 24:49

Spirit. He then trained them and sent them out to preach the good news and establish churches throughout Roman Asia.[20] New Testament revival is not complete without Spirit-empowered evangelism, missions, and church planting. This is the clear pattern presented in Scripture.

As we seek God for an outpouring of His Spirit, we must be ever mindful that Pentecostal revival is not only birthed in prayer, it is sustained by prayer. Therefore, when God does respond, and begins to pour out His Spirit on us, we must not interpret this development as a signal to slacken our efforts in prayer. We should rather allow it to inspire us to pray more. Like Timothy, we must "fan into flame" the gift of God's Spirit in us.[21] We do this through Spirit-anointed prayer.[22]

It is encouraging to know that when the Spirit comes, He will empower us and enable us to pray with even greater effectiveness. Paul describes how this works:

> "Likewise the Spirit helps us in our weakness. For we do not know what to pray for as we ought, but the Spirit himself intercedes for us with groanings too deep for words. And he who searches hearts knows what is the mind of the Spirit, because the Spirit intercedes for the saints according to the will of God."[23]

In other words, the same Holy Spirit who empowers our witness will also empower our prayers. In Acts, the outpouring of the Spirit did not terminate the church's prayer times; it rather intensified them. Therefore, when the Spirit comes, we should redouble our prayers for an even greater outpouring of the Spirit. We must continue to pray for

---

[20] Acts 19:1-10. (This strategy is discussed in more detail in Chapter 5, "Planting the Spirit-Empowered Missionary Church" under the section, "The Acts Model.")
[21] 2 Timothy 1:6
[22] Ephesians 6:18
[23] Romans 8:26-27

the Spirit's guidance and for new believers to be empowered by the Spirit. And by all means, we must continue to proclaim the gospel to the lost in the power of the Holy Spirit.

Mobilize for Prayer

The prophet Joel told of a time when God would send a "latter rain" to the earth. He was speaking figuratively of a day when God would powerfully pour out His Spirit on all flesh.[24] Nine centuries later, on the Day of Pentecost, Peter announced that the day of fulfillment had at long last arrived. "This is what was uttered through the prophet Joel," he declared, "'And in the last days it shall be, God declares, that I will pour out my Spirit on all flesh, and your sons and your daughters shall prophesy.'"[25] The prophet Zechariah also spoke of the latter rain. He directed God's people to "ask the Lord for rain in the time of the latter rain."[26]

There is a lesson here for us. During these last days of time, when God is pouring out His Spirit on all flesh, we must never presume upon God's goodness. We must, rather, fervently pursue the promise of the Spirit through devoted prayer. According to the instructions of our Lord, we must "keep asking…keep seeking …[and] keep knocking"[27] in faith-filled intercession. If we will do this, God will keep His promise and freely pour out His Spirit on us. As we set ourselves to prayer for Pentecostal renewal, we must simultaneously mobilize our churches for corporate intercession. Here are six practical ways we can do this:

1. Teach and preach. If we seek authentic Pentecostal revival in our churches, we must teach and preach often on the subject. We must show our people what true Pentecostal revival looks like and

---

[24] Joel 2:23, 28 (KJV)
[25] Acts 2:16-17
[26] Zechariah 10:1 (KJV)
[27] Luke 11:9 (literal translation)

what it will require of them. We must then call them to committed prayer for the Spirit and lead them into personal witness, church planting and missions.[28]

2. Pray during church services. Prayer for the Spirit during regular church services will help keep the need for Pentecostal revival before the people. We could preface these mini prayer events with brief explanations of what the revival will look like when it comes. During this time, it would be good for the people to ask God to empower them as His witnesses by filling and refilling them with His Spirit.

3. Scheduled times of corporate prayer and fasting. The church will also want to schedule special days or weeks of prayer and fasting. During these times of spiritual emphasis, the people could pray for revival and commit themselves more fully to God's mission. It may be good to schedule early morning, noontime, and evening prayer sessions during these times. Overnight prayer meetings may also be scheduled on weekends and holidays.

4. Prayer retreats. At appropriate times, the church may want to schedule prayer retreats when the people go away to a special place to pray and seek God's face. I remember my years in Malawi when I observed how some churches in Lilongwe occasionally took their people to nearby Bunda Mountain for prayer retreats. Such prayer retreats could include times of exhortation, worship, and intense intercessory prayer.

5. Special prayer groups. Certain people in the church will feel that God is calling them to a ministry of intercessory prayer. The church will want to organize these people into special prayer groups. These intercessors can meet regularly to pray for Pentecostal revival

---

[28] The e-book, *Interceding for the Nations: 100 Sermon Outlines on Missional Prayer,* is available for free download at www.DecadeofPentecost.org

and other needs in the church. The church will also want to organize prayer teams of men, women, youth, and even children.

6. *Mobilize for outreach.* As we organize for prayer, we should, at the same time, mobilize for evangelistic outreach. We could schedule open-air services in the markets and times of door-to-door witnessing in the neighborhoods. The leadership of the church will also want to mobilize the people for church planting. Prayerfully choose a place that needs a Spirit-filled church. Then, begin to intercede for that place. When the time is right, lead a team into that area to plant the new church. A truly Spirit-filled church should also receive a monthly missions offering to send missionaries to unreached peoples and places.

Review and Application

Prayer is a key to true Pentecostal revival and successful missions outreach. Now that you have completed this lesson, take time to commit yourself to pray until God pours out His Spirit on you and your church.

Reflect:

Reflect on the following issues:

- Describe how the book of Acts relates prayer to the outpouring of the Spirit.
- Discuss the relationship between prayer, the baptism in the Holy Spirit, and revival.

Apply:

Now, make the following applications to your present ministry:

- Honestly assess the spiritual state of your church as it relates to true revival as portrayed in the book of Acts.
- Develop a strategy for leading your church or ministry into Pentecostal revival. (Note: Your strategy should include prayer and an emphasis on Spirit-baptism.)

Commit:

Finally, pray this prayer and make this commitment:

- *Prayer:* "Oh Lord, pour out your Spirit on me and on my church, filling us and empowering us as your witnesses at home and to the ends of the earth."
- *Commitment:* "Lord, I commit myself to you and your mission in the earth. I will pray daily for an outpouring of the Spirit on Africa, my country, and my church."

Notes:

~ Chapter 5 ~

PLANTING THE SPIRIT-EMPOWERED MISSIONARY CHURCH

Christ has commissioned His church to "go…and make disciples of all nations…teaching them to observe all that I have commanded."[1] Making disciples and teaching them to obey Christ's commands demands that we do more than simply "get people saved." It requires that we plant churches, for it is in the context of God's people gathered as the church that converts are taught and disciples are made.

This process is demonstrated in the teaching ministry of Paul and Barnabas in Antioch. Luke writes, "For a whole year they met with the church and taught a great many people."[2] It was in this context that disciples first came to be called Christians—that is, those who are

---

[1] Matthew 28:19
[2] Acts 11:26

like Christ. The Antioch church was the first to intentionally deploy Christian missionaries to the field.[3]

In Chapter 3, we stated that authentic Pentecostals employ the same methods as did the church in the book of Acts. We noted that one of those methods is planting Spirit-empowered missionary churches. In this lesson, we will enlarge on this subject.

As we consider our obligation to plant churches, an important question arises: "As we go out to plant new churches, *what kind* of churches shall we plant?" Shall we plant weak, dependent, "crying" churches, that is, churches that are always needing help? Or, shall we plant strong, self-reliant, reproducing churches? I suggest we plant the latter. We call these churches *Spirit-empowered missionary churches*. Where shall we look for a model of such churches? As we have done in previous chapters, we find our model in the book of Acts.

The Acts Model

As suggested above, the Acts model of a healthy church is a Spirit-empowered missionary church. Jesus mandated such churches in His final giving of the Great Commission in Acts 1:8, where He said, "You will receive power when the Holy Spirit has come upon you, and you will be my witnesses in Jerusalem and in all Judea and Samaria, and to the end of the earth." This statement of Jesus suggests two characteristics of the kind of churches Jesus intends for us to plant:

- *They must be empowered by the Spirit:* "You will receive power when the Holy Spirit comes on you."
- *They must be focused on the mission of God:* "You will be my witnesses…to the ends of the earth."

---

[3] Acts 13:1-3

This insight suggests that, when we go out to plant new churches, we should *intentionally* plant churches with these two characteristics. They should be Spirit-empowered, and they should be missional. In other words, we must plant churches that will soon be able to plant other Spirit-empowered missionary churches. This "Strategy of the Spirit" will result in a spontaneous multiplication of churches as happened in the book of Acts.

Like Paul in Acts, as we go into new areas, we would do well to plant churches in strategic locations. For example, Paul planted churches in centers of influence such as Athens, Corinth, and Ephesus.[4] We should do the same. However, before we plant these churches, we must ask an important question: "What is the point of planting churches in strategic locations if those churches do not have the spiritual vitality required to reproduce themselves and plant other like-minded churches?"

We have watched missions committees work hard to plant churches in strategic trading centers in their countries, only to have those new churches struggle to stay alive. These feeble churches need constant care from the mother church simply to survive. What is the wisdom in that? Christ rather wants us to plant churches that will multiply themselves by planting other lively churches in the towns and villages around them. In other words, we must plant churches that are spiritually vibrant, outwardly focused, and able to impact their communities and the world for Christ.

The Examples of Jesus and the Apostles

By planting Spirit-empowered missionary churches, we are following the biblical pattern, for Jesus himself very deliberately planted such a church. He proclaimed the gospel, called disciples, taught them about His mission, ensured that they were empowered by the Spirit, and sent them out to do the same. They were to begin in

---

[4] Athens (Acts 17:16-34); Corinth (18:1-18); Ephesus (19:1-41)

Jerusalem (their hometown) and continue to expand until they reached the ends of the earth.

The apostles followed Jesus' example. Like Him, they intentionally planted Spirit-empowered missionary churches. For instance, when the apostles at Jerusalem heard that a new church had been planted in Samaria, they immediately sent Peter and John to them to pray with them that they might receive the Holy Spirit.[5] Just as Jesus had insisted that His disciples be empowered by the Holy Spirit, the apostles now insisted that the Samaritans receive the same empowering.

Concerning the Samaritans, the Bible says that the Holy Spirit "had not yet fallen on any of them" according the Jesus' promise in Acts 1:8. The apostles looked on this situation with alarm. They knew that, if the gospel was to proceed from Samaria to the surrounding areas, these new believers would need to be empowered by the Holy Spirit. They, therefore, sent Peter and John to Samaria to pray with them to be filled with the Spirit.

When the apostles laid hands on them, they received the Holy Spirit. As a result, they were empowered by the Holy Spirit, and the church in Samaria became a powerful witnessing community. Just as Jesus had predicted, the gospel continued to expand, and churches continued to multiply throughout the region, for Luke tells us, "The church throughout all Judea and Galilee *and Samaria*...multiplied."[6] The principle is this: Anywhere the gospel goes *to,* it must go *from.* And for it to go powerfully from a place, the believers in that place must be empowered by the Spirit.

Paul used the same strategy in Ephesus.[7] When arriving in the city, his intention was to reach not only Ephesus but all of the Roman province of Asia with the gospel. This task would require a Spirit-

---

[5] Acts 8:17-18
[6] Acts 9:31 (emphasis added): cf. 15:3
[7] Act 19:1-10

empowered missionary church in Ephesus to serve as a base. Therefore, when Paul encountered twelve local disciples, he immediately asked them, "Did you receive the Holy Spirit when you believed?" If these men were to effectively participate in the mission, they would need to be empowered by the Spirit just as were the first disciples in Jerusalem. Paul then laid his hands on them, and "the Holy Spirit came on them, and they began speaking in tongues and prophesying."[8]

Once the apostle saw that they had been empowered by the Spirit, he mobilized them and sent them out to proclaim the good news and to plant other Spirit-empowered missionary churches throughout the region. Jesus and the apostles thus established a pattern for church expansion we must follow today. We too must go out and plant Spirit-empowered missionary churches.

The Importance of Intentionality

As we go out to plant new churches, it is important that we proceed with calculated *intentionality*. In other words, we must purposely plant churches that are empowered by the Spirit and committed to fulfilling God's mission. How foolish we would be to assume that, just because we are Pentecostal in name, the churches we plant will be Pentecostal in practice. Placing an "Assemblies of God" sign on a church does not automatically make it a Pentecostal church. And belonging to a missionary movement like the Assemblies of God does not ensure that the churches we plant will be missionally committed. Such thinking will inevitably lead to disappointment.

If we are to plant authentically Pentecostal churches, as described in Chapter 3, we must move with well-considered purpose. Our every decision must be intentional, and our every action deliberate. All must be aimed at producing a predetermined result—that is, a Spirit-empowered missionary church, a church that preaches the same

---

[8] Acts 19:6

message, shares the same mission, embraces the same experiences, and employs the same methods as did the church in the book of Acts. In short order, the churches we plant must be able to reproduce themselves by planting other Spirit-empowered missionary churches.

A Way Forward

How then can we ensure that we plant such churches? We must begin by having a clear picture in our minds of what we want the new church to look like. We want it to be a church where the members are full of the Holy Spirit and committed to the mission of God. We want a church that will very soon be planting other churches. We want a church that will, from the very beginning, participate in the missions program of the national church through committed prayer and generous missions giving. Only by planting such churches will we be able to launch an effective church planting movement, as did Paul in Ephesus.

Once we have in our minds a clear picture of the church we want to plant, we must move to implement deliberate strategies to ensure such a church emerges.

1. A Spirit-empowered church. The church planter aiming to establish a Spirit-empowered missionary church must ensure that he or she have themselves been baptized in the Holy Spirit, and that they are presently living "in step with the Spirit."[9] Further, the church planter must ensure that anyone who will take a lead role in the new church is filled with the Spirit. This is especially true of the man or woman who will remain to nurture the new church. How can one expect the church to be Spirit-empowered if the leadership of the church is not living and ministering in the Spirit's power? Again, this is how Jesus went about planting His church. It is also how Paul and

---

[9] Galatians 5:25 (NIV)

the other apostles went about planting new churches. They ministered in the Spirit's power and insisted that their disciples do the same.

Further, if we are to plant truly Spirit-empowered missionary churches, the pastor and other leaders must preach and teach often on the baptism in the Holy Spirit and the Spirit-empowered life. They must carefully explain to the people that the primary reason each of them needs to be empowered by the Spirit is so that they may effectively participate in God's mission.[10] Leaders should further pray with the people, giving them frequent opportunities to be filled and refilled with the Spirit. All along, through committed prayer, worship, and holy living, leaders must contend for the Spirit's presence in the church's gatherings.

2. A missionary church. From the very onset of the church, the new pastor must purposefully teach his or her people about God's mission to reconcile all people unto himself through faith in Jesus Christ. They must further teach them that the church exists to fulfill God's mission. In addition, the people must understand that Christ has personally commissioned each of them to do his or her part to advance God's mission through committed prayer, faithful witness, and generous giving.

Also, early on in the founding of the church, the pastor should form a missions committee. He should prayerfully choose those who will serve on the committee, looking for those who have been filled with the Spirit and display a zeal to do God's will. The missions committee will oversee and promote the evangelistic, church planting, and missions outreaches of the church. The pastor should meet regularly with his committee for teaching, prayer, and strategic planning. The missions-minded pastor will also receive regular offerings to fund the missions outreaches of the church. He should also lead the new congregation to participate in the foreign and home missions program of their national church.

---

[10] Acts 1:8

3. A church planting church. Finally, from the beginning, the church planter should inform the congregation, "This new church will be a special kind of church. It will be a Spirit-empowered missionary church, a church that plants other Spirit-empowered missionary churches." Then, along with select church leaders, the pastor should begin to survey the surrounding area for places that need a new church. Once these places are identified, the pastor can then lead the congregation in ongoing prayer for these places. Very soon, the missions committee should choose a location, and a church planting effort should be launched.

In preparation for the effort, the pastor will want to recruit and train members to participate. In addition, the pastor must preach and teach often on the call of God. In time, God will begin to raise up workers. Finally, when the time is right, the church should move out in faith to plant the new church. If the church planter will do these things, he or she can expect success. God will intervene, and a powerful Spirit-empowered church will emerge, a church that will in turn plant other like-minded churches.

Allow me to share an example of how we applied this strategy at the Assemblies of God School of Theology[11] in Lilongwe, Malawi, where I served for 14 years. Several times each year faculty members led students out to plant new churches. These church planting efforts usually took place from Friday evening through Sunday morning. The church planting team would typically arrive at the chosen locale on Friday afternoon. Upon arrival, some would begin preparing the site (often a schoolyard) for the evening service. Others would fan out into the community sharing the gospel and announcing the meeting to all.

In the Friday evening service, the students would sing and share personal testimonies. Then, someone would preach the gospel, ending the message with an invitation for the people to commit their lives to

---

[11] Now, the Malawi Assemblies of God Institute of Theology (MAGIT)

Christ. Always, someone responded and came forward for prayer. Before the evening activities closed, we would show the first half of the Jesus Film with a promise that we would show the second half the next evening.

Saturday morning was given to intercessory prayer, followed by house-to-house witnessing. Then, after a simple lunch, witnessing resumed into the mid-afternoon. The Saturday evening service followed the pattern of the Friday service, and several more would commit themselves to Christ. The last half of the Jesus Film was then shown. Finally, at the close of the service, someone would announce, "Tomorrow morning we will launch a new Assemblies of God church in a classroom of this school (or some other designated place)." We would then present one of the students to the congregation, announcing, "This man will be your new pastor." The pastor would conclude the meeting by inviting everyone to attend the new church the next morning.

On Sunday morning, several local people, including some of the new believers, would gather with the students for the church's inaugural service. Immediately, we began to implement our strategy for establishing a truly Pentecostal church. We would announce, "This new church will be a special kind of church. It will be the kind of church we read about in the Bible—a Spirit-empowered missionary church!" Then, using the Bible, we explained to the congregation just what that meant.

When it came time to receive the first offering, we announced, "Because this is going to be a missionary church, and because it will be a church planting church, our first offering will be to raise funds to plant another church very soon." Often, on hearing this, the people would begin to clap their hands in excitement. Although this offering was typically very modest, we felt that it was important to help the people understand their responsibility to reach others with the gospel.

When time came for the first sermon in the new church, we would take our text from Acts 1:8 and preached a simple message on the baptism in the Holy Spirit. We explained to the people their need to be empowered by the Holy Spirit in order to truly live for God and to fulfill His mission. We then called on people to come forward and commit themselves to God's mission and to be empowered by the Holy Spirit. Invariably, some were filled with the Spirit, speaking in tongues as the Spirit enabled them. The new pastor was expected to continue with this emphasis. We did these things to ensure that from the very beginning, the new church was infused with the DNA of a Spirit-empowered missionary church.

Paul instructed Timothy, his son in the faith, "What you have heard from me in the presence of many witnesses entrust to faithful men who will be able to teach others also."[12] This is the method the apostle employed in Ephesus where he intentionally planted a Spirit-empowered missionary church. When he found twelve disciples, after ensuring that they had been empowered by the Holy Spirit, he entrusted to them his understanding of God's kingdom and how it should advance into the surrounding region. He then sent them out to apply the same strategy in cities throughout Roman Asia. We know this because the Bible tells us, "This continued for two years, so that all the residents of Asia heard the word of the Lord, both Jews and Greeks."[13] This is a pattern we must follow today.

Review and Application

Now that you have completed this lesson, take a few moments to reflect, apply, and implement the things you have learned.

Reflect:

Reflect on the following issues:

---

[12] 2 Timothy 2:2
[13] Acts 19:10

- Describe the two key characteristics of a Spirit-empowered missionary church as presented in the book of Acts.
- Discuss what it means to *intentionally* plant a Spirit-empowered missionary church.

Apply:

Now, make the following applications to your present ministry:

- Evaluate the current state of your church or ministry in regards to church planting. How well are you doing? What changes do you need to make to ensure that your church planting efforts are more fruitful?
- Based on what you have learned in this lesson, what would you do to ensure that the next church you plant is a Spirit-empowered missionary church?

Commit:

Finally, pray this prayer and make this commitment:

- *Prayer:* "Lord, you purposefully planted a Spirit-empowered missionary church. The apostles followed in your footsteps and did the same. I ask you today, put into my heart that same desire and determination."
- *Commitment:* "I commit to leading my church in planting other Spirit-empowered missionary churches."

Notes:

~ Chapter 6 ~

LEADING A CHURCH INTO PENTECOSTAL REVIVAL[1]

In the last lesson, we discussed planting Spirit-empowered missionary churches. We believe this to be the responsibility of every truly Pentecostal church. For every place the gospel goes *to,* it must go *from.* It stands to reason, however, that before a church can plant another authentically Pentecostal church, it must itself be authentically Pentecostal. In this lesson, we will address this issue. We will investigate how we, as Pentecostal leaders, may lead our churches into Pentecostal revival.

Defining Revival

The first requisite in leading a church into authentic Pentecostal revival is for the pastor and people to have in their minds a clear picture of what real New Testament revival looks like. Sadly, however, many Pentecostal leaders have a wrong concept of revival. They have gotten their idea of revival, not from Scripture, but from

---

[1] This lesson was originally developed by AIA team member, Mark R. Turney. Most of what is said here are his thoughts on the subject.

popular church culture. They thus envision revival as a church filled with people joyfully singing, dancing, and praising God. Others think of revival as God showering prosperity and material blessing on His people. While some of these experiences may accompany revival, they in no way describe true revival as pictured in the Bible—particularly in the book of Acts. This New Testament book vividly describes how the church's first revivals took place. From it, we a get a clear concept of what an authentic Pentecostal revival looks like.

As we noted in Chapter 4, the word *revival* is not found in the New Testament. However, the concept of spiritual renewal is. Revival speaks of renewed life and implies the restoration of consciousness, vigor, and strength. What the Old Testament calls revival,[2] the New Testament describes as an outpouring of the Spirit.[3] In the first two chapters of Acts, Luke identifies three essential elements in revival. These are three results we can expect when true Pentecostal revival occurs. First, God's people will be baptized in—and thus empowered by—the Holy Spirit.[4] Next, God's people will begin to boldly proclaim Christ to the lost.[5] Finally, lost people will repent, put their faith in Christ, and be saved.[6]

The book of Acts reveals several other outcomes of a genuine outpouring of the Holy Spirit, including signs, wonders, healings, and other miracles.[7] These occurrences often result in great joy, lively church gatherings, and church growth. However, baptism in the Holy Spirit, powerful witness, and people coming to Christ are the three essential elements of any authentic Pentecostal revival. If any of these elements are missing, true revival has not yet taken place.

---

[2] Psalm 85:6; Habakkuk 3:2
[3] Acts 2:17-18
[4] Acts 1:8; 2:1-4
[5] Acts 2:14-40; 4:31
[6] Acts 2:41, 47; 5:12-16
[7] Acts 2:43; 5:12-16

A Biblical Example

Let's look more closely at our biblical example of revival recorded in Acts 2. In this passage, we observe the three essential elements of true revival just mentioned, as well as four more elements naturally related to these three:

1. The people seek God. At the close of his gospel, Luke tells us that, in preparation for the outpouring of the Spirit at Pentecost, the disciples "were continually in the temple blessing God."[8] In beginning the book of Acts, He informs us that they "with one accord were devoting themselves to prayer."[9] The seeds of Pentecostal revival are thus sown in prayer.

2. God pours out His Spirit. Every revival begins with an outpouring of God's Spirit. At Pentecost, it happened like this:

> "And suddenly there came from heaven a sound like a mighty rushing wind, and it filled the entire house where they were sitting. And divided tongues as of fire appeared to them and rested on each one of them."[10]

Peter interpreted the event by quoting the prophet Joel, who described what was happening as an outpouring of God's Spirit.[11]

3. Believers receive the Spirit. It is one thing for God to pour out His Spirit; it is quite another for His people to receive the Spirit. On the Day of Pentecost, the Holy Spirit first came upon the 120 disciples, just as Jesus had promised.[12] They were then, "all filled with the Holy Spirit and began to speak in other tongues as the Spirit

---

[8] Luke 24:53
[9] Acts 1:14
[10] Acts 2:2-3
[11] Acts 2:17
[12] Acts 1:8; 2:3

gave them utterance."[13] At that moment, they received power to be Christ's witnesses at home and to the ends of the earth.

4. Outsiders take notice. The disciples' receiving the Spirit did not go unnoticed. At Pentecost, the crowd saw the disciples being filled with the Spirit and heard them miraculously speaking in unlearned languages. This experience made a profound impact on them. The Bible says, "And all were amazed and perplexed, saying to one another, 'What does this mean?'"[14]

5. The gospel is proclaimed. Now, full of the Holy Spirit, Peter observed the gathering crowd and perceived that they were ready to hear the gospel. Embolden by the Spirit, he told them about Jesus and called them to repentance and faith.[15]

6. Many respond and are saved. Because of the outpouring of the Holy Spirit, and Peter's anointed proclamation of the gospel, many responded and were saved. The Bible says that the listeners were "cut to the heart" and cried out to Peter, "What shall we do?" The apostle responded, "Repent and be baptized every one of you in the name of Jesus Christ for the forgiveness of your sins, and you will receive the gift of the Holy Spirit."[16] As a result, 3,000 were saved, baptized in water, and added to the church. The context further implies that these same people were baptized in the Holy Spirit and empowered as Christ's witnesses according to Jesus' promise in Acts 1:8.

7. The church expands. Following Pentecost (and other outpourings of the Spirit throughout Acts), the church continued to grow numerically and expand geographically. Luke describes this repeated cycle of revival:

> "And they devoted themselves to the apostles' teaching and the fellowship, to the breaking of bread and the prayers. And

---

[13] Acts 2:4
[14] Acts 2:12
[15] Acts 2:14-40
[16] Acts 2:37-38

awe came upon every soul, and many wonders and signs were being done through the apostles. And all who believed were together and had all things in common. And they were selling their possessions and belongings and distributing the proceeds to all, as any had need. And day by day, attending the temple together and breaking bread in their homes, they received their food with glad and generous hearts, praising God and having favor with all the people. And the Lord added to their number day by day those who were being saved."[17]

Other evidences of revival revealed in this passage are devotion to Scripture, prayer, and love for one another. Additionally, the people were filled with a sense of awe as God performed wonders in their midst. The presence of the Spirit further created in their hearts an attitude of generosity. These things resulted in ongoing church growth as "day by day the Lord added to their number those who were being saved."

In summary, true Pentecostal revival happens as people believe the message about Jesus, are filled with the Spirit, and then go out to share the good news with others, who are themselves saved, filled with the Spirit, and become faithful proclaimers of the gospel. As this process is repeated over and over, the revival spreads far and wide. Or, in the words of Jesus, it occurs "in Jerusalem and all Judea and Samaria, and to the end of the earth."[18] This is the sort of revival we seek.

The Role of the Leader

The church lives in continual need of revival. Just as the body will die if it stops breathing air, the church will die if it stops "breathing in" the Spirit. Jesus reminds us, "It is the Spirit who gives

---

[17] Acts 2:42-47; cf. 4:31-35; 5:
[18] Acts 1:8

life; the flesh is no help at all."[19] You will remember, in Chapter 2 we stated that no Pentecostal church can endure as a truly Pentecostal church without experiencing frequent outpourings of the Holy Spirit. It is therefore essential that every Pentecostal pastor encourage his or her members to persist in prayer for fresh outpourings of the Spirit.

Speaking of the Holy Spirit, Jesus told His disciples, "I tell you, ask, and it will be given to you; seek, and you will find; knock, and it will be opened to you."[20] The Holman Christian Standard Bible translates Jesus words more literally: "I say to you, *keep asking,* and it will be given to you. *Keep searching,* and you will find. *Keep knocking,* and the door will be opened to you."[21] The implication is that, as long as we continue to ask, we will continue to receive from God. However, when we stop asking, we stop receiving. Thus, the fires of Pentecostal revival must be fueled by unremitting prayer.

Further, the Pentecostal pastor must teach his or her people how to pray in faith. They must come to believe that, if they will faithfully seek God, He will keep His promise and send revival.[22] The pastor will do well to continually remind the people of Peter's prophetic declaration: "In the last days, God says, I *will* pour out my Spirit on all people."[23] As Christians embrace this promise, they will be encouraged to confidently heed the prophet's exhortation: "Ask the Lord for rain in the time of the latter rain,"[24] and to believe Jesus' promise: "The heavenly Father [will] give the Holy Spirit to those who ask him!"[25]

---

[19] John 6:63

[20] Luke 11:9; cf. v. 13

[21] Nashville, TN: Holman Bible Publishers, 2009 (emphasis added)

[22] Mark 11:24

[23] Acts 2:17 (emphasis added)

[24] Zechariah 10:1 (NKJV)

[25] Luke 11:13

As we pursue Pentecostal revival, we must, at the same time, pursue Pentecostal mission. This was Jesus' clear mandate in Acts 1:8. First, *He promised revival*: "You will receive power when the Holy Spirit comes on you." In the same breath, *He mandated mission:* "And you will be my witnesses...to the ends of the earth." Therefore, the task of leading believers into Spirit-baptism, and then into Spirit-empowered witness, must remain a top priority for any Pentecostal pastor. He or she must be ever mindful that a chief reason God places leaders in local churches is that they may raise up other Spirit-empowered disciples whom He can use to build His kingdom.[26]

It is therefore essential that the Pentecostal pastor know how to lead his or her church into authentic New Testament revival with the aim of at mobilizing them for Spirit-empowered mission.

Some Practical Advice

In Acts 8, Luke tells of another mighty revival that occurred a few weeks after Pentecost. This outpouring happened about 35 miles north of Jerusalem in the neighboring province of Samaria.[27] From this revival, we can garner some additional strategies Pentecostal pastors and other leaders can employ to encourage revival in their churches. Let's look at seven of those strategies:

1. Be personally filled. The first step in leading one's church into revival is for the pastor and other leaders of the church to themselves experience revival. They can do this by earnestly seeking to be filled with, and remain full of, the Holy Spirit themselves. Philip, who led the Samaritan revival, was one of the Spirit-filled "deacons" in the Jerusalem church.[28] He was likely filled with the Spirit on the Day of Pentecost or soon after. When he was driven out of the city by persecution, he remained full of the Holy Spirit, and upon arriving in

---

[26] Ephesians 4:11-12
[27] You can read about this revival in Acts 8:1-25.
[28] Acts 6:3-5

Samaria, he ministered in the Spirit's power. A mighty revival ensued.

The same can be said of the Spirit-filled believers who fled to Syrian Antioch. The Bible says, "The hand of the Lord was with them, and a great number who believed turned to the Lord."[29] The *hand of the Lord* in this passage refers to the anointing of the Spirit that was on their lives. Years later, Paul, who was himself full of the Holy Spirit, sparked a Pentecostal revival in Ephesus by praying for twelve disciples to be filled with the Spirit.[30] Philip and Paul were able to inspire revival in their churches because they themselves were full of the Holy Spirit.

2. Exercise bold faith. When Philip arrived in Samaria, he acted in bold faith. As a result, God gave him miracles to confirm the message he preached, and many were won to the Lord. We too must believe that revival is possible, and we must act on that belief. Like Abraham, we must "be fully persuaded that God has power to do what He has promised."[31] So, start right now. Boldly act on the promises of God with full assurance that revival is coming. Your faith will be contagious. When others see it, they too will be encouraged to believe God for revival.

3. Proclaim Christ. The Bible tells us, "Philip went down to the city of Samaria and proclaimed to them the Christ."[32] This was the practice of Christians in Acts. Wherever they went, they told people about Jesus.[33] If we want authentic Pentecostal revival in our churches, we must do the same. We must boldly proclaim Christ to all.

---

[29] Acts 11:21
[30] Acts 19:1-7
[31] Romans 4:21 (paraphrased)
[32] Acts 8:5
[33] Cf. Acts 2:22; 3:13; 4:2, 33; 9:22; 16:31

Chapter 6: Leading a Church into Pentecostal Revival

4. Expect confirmation. As we preach and talk about Christ, we should trust God to confirm the word with signs following. Luke tells us that, as Philip preached, "The crowds with one accord paid attention to what was being said...when they heard him and saw the signs that he did."[34] These miraculous signs included powerful deliverances and miraculous healings. As a result, great joy came to the people, many were saved, and revival came to the city.

5. Emphasize Spirit baptism. When the apostles at Jerusalem heard that the Samaritans had received the gospel, they sent Peter and John to pray with them to be filled with the Spirit.[35] We too, if we want to experience true Pentecostal revival, must teach and preach on Spirit baptism. And we must pray with people to receive the Spirit. This will help prepare them to fully participate in the revival and to spread the gospel to the lost.

6. Lead in witnessing. Philip launched the Samaritan revival through bold Spirit-empowered witness to the lost people of Samaria. In doing this, he became an example to the people. We know they followed his example in witnessing, for within a short time, "the church throughout...Samaria had peace and was being built up. And walking in the fear of the Lord and in the comfort of the Holy Spirit, it multiplied."[36] If we want genuine spiritual revival in our churches, we must follow Philip's example. We must not only tell our people to witness, we must be an example of the true purpose of Pentecostal revival by being a witness ourselves. Remember Jesus' promise: "But you will receive power when the Holy Spirit has come upon you, and you will be my witnesses..."[37]

7. Persist in prayer. Finally, if we are to move our churches from dormancy to Pentecostal revival, we must pray. The Bible tells us that

---

[34] Acts 8:6
[35] Acts 8:14-17
[36] Acts 9:31
[37] Acts 1:8

when the apostles Peter and John arrived in Samaria, they "prayed for them that they might receive the Holy Spirit."[38] Throughout Acts, Luke connects prayer to the outpouring of the Spirit.[39] If we want to see authentic Pentecostal revival in our churches, we too must pray. And we must persist until the answer comes, remembering the words of Paul, "Let us not grow weary of doing good, for in due season we will reap, if we do not give up."[40]

Review and Application

Now that you have completed this lesson, take a few moments to reflect, apply, and implement the things you have learned.

Reflect:

Reflect on the following issues:

- List and discuss the three essential results of authentic Pentecostal revival as presented in Acts 1-2.
- Discuss the relationship between Spirit baptism and true New Testament revival.

Apply:

Now, make the following applications to your present ministry:

- Evaluate the present spiritual condition of your church based on the following three characteristics of authentic Pentecostal revival:

  1. The Spirit is being poured out and people are being filled with the Spirit.
  2. The gospel is being clearly proclaimed both in the church and in the community.

---

[38] Acts 8:15 (emphasis added)
[39] For more on this, see Chapter 4, "Prayer and Pentecostal Revival."
[40] Galatians 6:9

3. People are regularly being won to Christ.

- Develop a plan to lead your church into authentic Pentecostal revival.

Commit:

As we close this lesson, let's commit ourselves to doing whatever is required to bring true Pentecostal revival into our churches.

- *Prayer:* "Lord, I offer myself and my church to you. Take me and fill me with your Holy Spirit. Enable me to lead my people into an authentic Pentecostal revival, the kind we read about in the book of Acts."
- *Commitment:* "I commit to do whatever is necessary to lead my church into authentic Pentecostal revival and Spirit-empowered witness to the lost."

Notes:

~ Chapter 7 ~

How to Preach on the Baptism in the Holy Spirit

In previous lessons, we have emphasized the importance of God's missionary people being empowered by the Holy Spirit. This missional empowering is an essential first step in mobilizing the church for evangelism and missions. Through Spirit baptism, God gives His people the power to effectively advance His kingdom at home and to the ends of the earth. In this lesson, we will learn how we can teach and preach more effectively on this vital subject.

Four Preliminary Considerations

Understanding four foundational concepts concerning Spirit baptism will help prepare us to develop more convincing sermons and to preach more effectively on the subject.[1]

1. Must be a priority. Mobilizing the church for effective witness is a primary responsibility of every pastor. The first step of that process is ensuring that God's people have been empowered by the Holy Spirit. To accomplish this, the pastor will need to preach often and effectively on the subject. Both Jesus and the apostles prioritized preaching and teaching on Spirit baptism. Jesus especially stressed the issue during His final 40 days on earth. As He was preparing the church for their impending mission, He spoke often of the Spirit's empowering.[2] He commanded His disciples, "Stay in the city until you are clothed with power from on high."[3]

The apostles also prioritized preaching and teaching on Spirit baptism. For instance, in his Pentecost sermon, Peter stressed the empowering work of the Holy Spirit. Although he was preaching in an evangelistic setting, he spoke of the work of the Spirit in 10 of 25 verses (40%) of his message.[4] This emphasis on the work of the Spirit continued with Peter and the other apostles and evangelists throughout the book of Acts.[5]

Jesus revealed the primary purpose of Spirit baptism when He told His disciples, "You will receive power...and you will be my

---

[1] The Acts in Africa Initiative has developed the book, *Proclaiming Pentecost: 100 Sermon Outlines on Spirit-Empowered Missions,* to assist pastors in this area. It is available at www.DecadeofPentecost.org.

[2] See Mark 16:18-19; Luke 24:44-49; John 20:21-22; Acts 1:4-8

[3] Luke 24:49

[4] Acts 2:14-18; 32-33; 37-39

[5] I.e., Peter and John in Samaria (Acts 8:14-18); Peter in Caesarea (Acts 10:38, 44-45); and Paul in Ephesus (Acts 19:1-6)

witnesses…to the end of the earth."[6] When we understand the missional purpose of the experience, it becomes clear why Jesus and the apostles insisted that every follower of Christ be baptized in the Holy Spirit.

2. Context matters. The culture of the church community in which one is filled with the Spirit will significantly affect how he or she receives and lives out the Pentecostal experience. The proper scriptural context for receiving the Spirit is preparation for, and participation in, God's mission. This is what happened in the book of Acts. At Pentecost, the early disciples received the Spirit on their way to fulfilling Christ's command to be His witnesses to the ends of the earth. Later, Peter declared that God freely gives the Spirit to those who obey God by faithfully proclaiming Christ to the lost.[7]

When God's people receive Spirit baptism in a context where they clearly understand the purpose of the experience, and are committed to fulfilling God's mission, a powerful missional synergy occurs. The same will happen today if we will call people to be filled with the Spirit in preparation for witness, church planting, and missions.

3. Stay focused. As we preach on the baptism in the Holy Spirit, we must "keep our eyes on the prize." That is, we must remain focused on our goal of seeing believers empowered by the Holy Spirit and mobilized as effective witnesses for Jesus. Everything we say or do must contribute to our achieving that goal. Every word must be aimed at directing people to the altar to be empowered by the Spirit. To achieve this, we should keep our message short and to the point. We must then call the people to the altar to be filled with the Spirit.

4. Preach with faith. When we preach on the baptism in the Holy Spirit, we must hold to the belief that, if we will do our part, God will surely do His. We must trust Him to keep His promise and to baptize

---

[6] Acts 1:8
[7] Acts 5:32, cf. vv. 28-29

believers in the Holy Spirit. We must believe that Jesus will fulfill His promise concerning the Holy Spirit: "Ask, and it *will* be given you… for e*veryone* who asks receives…"[8]

Further, because we are moving in faith, we will not try to force the issue. We will confidently present the message, pray with seekers to be filled, and fully trust God to fill them with His Spirit. Having preached several hundred times on the baptism in the Holy Spirit, and having prayed with thousands to be filled, we at the Acts in Africa Initiative can assure you that God is faithful. He will fill hungry seekers with His Spirit. We must simply present the message and give them the opportunity.

Three Important Goals

Our preaching on the baptism in the Holy Spirit will be more effective if we will keep in mind three important goals we seek to achieve as we present the message:

1. Create desire. God gives His Spirit to those who desire a deeper relationship with Him and want to reach others for Christ. It is therefore important that the preacher endeavors to create such desire in the hearts of the hearers. Jesus spoke of this desire when He said, "Blessed are those who hunger and thirst for righteousness, for they will be filled."[9] On another occasion, speaking about the Holy Spirit, Jesus cried out to all who would hear, "If anyone thirsts, let him come to me and drink."[10]

There are three ways we can create this desire in people's hearts. First, we can show them how this experience with the Spirit will enrich their lives. Tell them how being baptized in the Holy Spirit

---

[8] Luke 11:9-10, (emphasis added)
[9] Matthew 5:6 (NIV)
[10] John 7:37

will result in an overflowing fullness of the Spirit,[11] a deepened reverence for God,[12] an intensified consecration to His work,[13] and a more active love for Christ, for His Word, and for the lost.[14] Also, show them how being baptized in the Spirit will empower them to be more effective witnesses for Christ. They will receive supernatural boldness to speak to the lost.[15] Along with this power to speak for Christ will come power to do the works of Christ and to challenge and defeat demonic spirits in His name.[16]

Finally, help your listeners picture themselves full of the Holy Spirit, living close to God, and winning the lost to Christ. You can do this by telling Bible stories and other stories from history of people whom the Spirit empowered and God used. Then, show them how God will use them in the same way. You may want to use the testimonies and stories of other Christians you know. And don't forget to share with them your personal testimony of being filled with the Spirit and how the experience has impacted your life. These things will help them see how God can use common people to do uncommon things for Him.

2. Inspire expectant faith. Scripture teaches that "[we] receive the promised Spirit through faith."[17] Jesus promised, "Whoever believes in me, as the Scripture has said, 'Out of his heart will flow rivers of living water.'"[18] Therefore, when we preach on the baptism in the Holy Spirit, our aim is to inspire expectant faith in the hearts of the hearers. Expectant faith is a state of mind and heart where people keenly anticipate that God is about to fulfill His promise in the

---

[11] John 7:37-39
[12] Acts 2:43; Hebrews 12:28-29
[13] Acts 2:42
[14] Mark 16:20; Romans 5:5
[15] Acts 1:8; 4:31
[16] John 14:12, 16; Matthew 12:28; Mark 16:16
[17] Galatians 3:14
[18] John 7:38

immediate present. Jesus spoke of this kind of faith when He said, "Whatever you ask in prayer, believe that you *have received* it, and it will be yours."[19] You can inspire such faith in your hearers in at least three ways:

First, remind them of the promises of Jesus: "Ask and it will be given to you...everyone who asks receives...the heavenly Father [will] give the Holy Spirit to those who ask him!"[20] Assure them that, if they will ask God out of a sincere heart, He will hear and answer their prayer.[21]

Second, remind them that the gift of the Spirit is for everyone. It is significant that in the book of Acts, each time the Spirit is poured out, everyone present is filled.[22] On the Day of Pentecost, "they were *all* filled with the Holy Spirit."[23] Peter then stood and encouraged the people, saying, "The promise is for you and for your children and *for all* who are far off, *everyone* whom the Lord our God calls to himself."[24] Assure your hearers that the promise of the Holy Spirit is for all God's children until Jesus comes again—including them!

Third, let your hearers know that God desires to give us His Spirit even more than we desire to receive. He is not withholding His gift, nor is He playing a game of hide-and-seek with us. If we are prepared to obey Christ and become His witnesses to the lost, God is prepared to empower us with His Spirit.[25]

3. Bring to clear understanding. A final goal we must keep in mind as we preach on the baptism in the Holy Spirit is that we seek to

---

[19] Mark 11:24 (emphasis added)
[20] Luke 11:9-13
[21] Cf. 1 John 5:14-15
[22] Cf. Acts 2:4; 4:31; 8:17; 10:44; 19:6
[23] Acts 2:4 (emphasis added)
[24] Acts 2:39 (emphasis added)
[25] Acts 5:32; cf. v. 29

bring our hearers into a clear understanding of what the experience is, and of how it is received. Let's look at each of these goals:

First, teach them what the baptism in the Holy Spirit is. Sadly, most Pentecostal Christians have no clear understanding of the true nature, purpose, and importance of the experience. We must, therefore, clearly explain these things to them. The baptism in the Holy Spirit is a powerful, life-changing encounter with God. Its purpose is to bring committed believers into a more intimate relationship with Him and to empower them to be witnesses for Christ. After being born again, the baptism in the Holy Spirit is the most important experience in the life of any Christian. It is so important that, just before returning to heaven, Jesus commanded His followers to be "clothed with power from on high."[26]

Next, teach them how the gift of the Spirit is received. It is received by asking, receiving, and speaking in faith.[27] It is not received by prolonged begging or weeping. Neither is the Spirit passed from one believer to another as one would pass on a piece of merchandise. The experience comes directly from heaven into the heart of the seeker.[28] It is a gift from the heavenly Father and from Jesus Himself.[29] It is received as the recipient exercises a bold, present tense, appropriating kind of faith. While laying on of hands can, and often does, inspire the seeker's faith, and help to facilitate the Spirit's presence upon the seeker, in the end, only Jesus can baptize in the Holy Spirit.[30]

---

[26] Luke 24:49; Acts 1:4-5; cf. Ephesians 5:18

[27] This procedure is discussed in Chapter 7, "Praying with Believers to Receive the Holy Spirit."

[28] Acts 2:2

[29] Luke 11:13; Acts 2:32-33

[30] Luke 3:16-17

The Sermon Itself

Our discussion now brings us to the sermon itself. Let's begin by talking about the nature and content of the sermon.

1. Keep it simple. One mistake preachers often make when preaching on the baptism in the Holy Spirit (or for that matter, on any biblical subject) is to over-complicate the issue. We should therefore resist any temptation of trying to impress the people with our knowledge of the subject. And by all means, we should not come with some "new revelation" from God. When we stand before the people, our goal is to simply and clearly tell them what the Bible says.

Step by step, tell the people what they must know and what they must do to receive the Spirit. In your message, aim at achieving three critical elements of good communication: *clarity* (your message should be easy to understand), *conciseness* (your message should be short and to the point), and *cogency* (your message should be strong and compelling).

2. Consider your content. In preaching on the baptism in the Holy Spirit, it helps to see the sermon as having two main parts. I call these two parts the message and the instructions.

The message refers to what we commonly think of as the sermon proper. During this part of the sermon, you will teach or preach on some pertinent biblical insight concerning the work of the Spirit in the life of the church or individual Christian. The message includes the text, the introduction, and body of the sermon. Time wise, it will make up about half of the sermon.

The instructions follow the message. They remain essentially the same in every sermon on Spirit baptism. Some would see this as part of the altar call or conclusion of the sermon; however, it is more than that. In the message, you sought to inspire people to be filled with the Spirit. Now in the instructions, you will tell them exactly what they must do to receive.

Chapter 7: How to Preach on the Baptism in the Holy Spirit

You may begin your instruction by saying, "You may be asking, 'Pastor, how can I receive this gift of the Holy Spirit that you've been preaching about? How can I be baptized in the Holy Spirit today?'" You then tell them as simply and as clearly as possible what they must do to receive the Spirit, and what they can expect to happen as they are receiving. Your instructions may proceed as follows:

"The gift of the Holy Spirit is received by simply asking in faith. Jesus said that the Spirit fills and flows into and through 'whoever believes.'[31] Paul taught that we 'receive the promised Spirit through faith.'[32]

"In a few moments, we will all come forward, and I will lead you in prayer. Together, we will take three steps of faith. We will *ask* in faith, *receive* by faith, and *speak* in faith. Let me explain what I mean.

"First, we will *ask in faith*. Jesus said, 'Ask and it will be given to you.'[33] He also said, 'Whatever you ask for in prayer, believe that you have received it, and it will be yours.'[34] So we will ask, and we will believe that God is answering our prayer. As we believe, we will sense the Holy Spirit coming upon us, just as He came upon the disciples in the book of Acts.[35] We will then wait in the Spirit's presence for a while. As we do this, open wide your spirit to the Spirit of God.

"Next, we will *receive by faith*. Jesus also said, 'Everyone who asks receives.'[36] He was not talking about passively receiving, as one might receive sunshine on his back. He is rather talking about actively reaching out in faith and taking the gift that God is offering. We do this by believing that we 'have received.' The moment you truly

---

[31] John 7:38
[32] Galatians 3:14; cf. v. 5
[33] Luke 11:9
[34] Mark 11:24
[35] Acts 1:8; 2:3, 17; 8:16; 10:44; 19:6
[36] Luke 11:10

believe that you have received the Spirit, He will rush into your being and fill you to overflowing. Again, if you will remain open and sensitive to God, you will sense the Spirit's presence deep within—in your 'innermost being.'[37]

"At this point, we will take our third step of faith. We will boldly *speak in faith*. The Bible says that on the Day of Pentecost 'they were all filled with the Holy Spirit *and began to speak...*' As they spoke, the Holy Spirit who had filled them now flowed through them, and out of them, inspiring and enabling them to 'speak in other tongues as the Spirit gave the utterance.'[38] You, too, will begin to speak in tongues as the Spirit gives the utterance. The speaking, however, will not come from your mind as in regular speech, but from deep inside, where you sense the presence of God. You will speak out of your spirit.[39] When this happens, don't be afraid; just yield yourself more and more to the Spirit of God. As you do, words will begin to flow from deep within you. It will be God's sign to you that He has empowered you to speak for Him."

Once you have completed your time of instruction, it is time to call the people forward to be filled and refilled with the Holy Spirit.

Delivering the Sermon

Sermon delivery is most effective when it includes three critical elements: anointing, passion, and authenticity. Let's look at each of those elements:

1. Anointing. Jesus ministered with an anointing (or touch of the Holy Spirit) on His life and words,[40] as did Peter and John,[41] the

---

[37] John 7:38 (NASB)

[38] Acts 2:4

[39] 1 Corinthians 14:2 (NASB)

[40] Luke 4:18-19; John 6:63

[41] Acts 4:8

apostles,[42] Stephen,[43] and Paul.[44] And so must we, if our words are to have maximum impact upon our hearers. As we preach, the people must sense that the Spirit of the Lord is upon us inspiring our thoughts and empowering our words.

2. Passion. Effective preaching is passionate preaching. And true passion arises from deep within one's being. It is a fervent gushing forth of the "well springs of the great deep" from a man or woman's soul. When we preach with passion, the people will hear it in our voices, see it in our eyes, and sense it in our words. Because of this anointed passion, as on the Day of Pentecost, the hearers will be "cut to the heart," and they will cry out—if not with their voices, at least in their spirits—"What must we do?"[45]

3. Authenticity. As we preach, we must resist any temptation to put on a show or to draw attention to ourselves. Rather, we must be like John the Baptist. When he introduced Jesus as the one who baptizes in the Holy Spirit, he reminded the people, "[He] is more powerful than I. I am not worthy to untie the strap of His sandals." He then added, "He must increase, but I must decrease."[46] So let it be with us as we preach on the baptism in the Holy Spirit. When the people sense that the preacher is authentic, and that he or she honestly seeks what is best for them, they are compelled to listen and to eagerly respond.

Extending the Altar Call

Once you have delivered the "message" and clearly presented the "instruction," it is time to proceed to the altar call. Everything you have said and done in your sermon has led to this point. It is now time

---

[42] Acts 4:33
[43] Acts 6:8, 10, 15
[44] Acts 13:9-11
[45] Acts 2:37, 40
[46] Luke 3:16, 30

to draw the net and call people to the front of the church to be filled with the Spirit. As you do this, it is good to keep the following ideas in mind:

1. Give clear instructions. As you extend the invitation, it is very important that you be very clear with your instructions. Often people fail to respond simply because they are confused about what the preacher wants them to do. Remember, they are already nervous about the prospect of going to the front of the church. Therefore, unclear, confusing instructions will further cause them to hold back. On the other hand, clear, easy-to-understand instructions will help to settle their minds concerning what they need to do. This will encourage them to respond and come forward. Your instructions may go something like this:

> "I'm going to ask those who want to be filled or refilled with the Spirit to step from where you are now seated, come to the front of the church, and stand in front of me. When you get here, I will lead you in a prayer to be filled with the Spirit."

Once the people arrive at the front of the church, briefly summarize the directions you gave to them during the "instructions" part of your sermon. Tell them how the prayer time will proceed, and how they will be expected to respond. If you will do these things, you will find more people responding to the altar call and being filled with the Spirit.

2. Call everyone to prayer. As you call people to the front of the church to be filled with the Spirit, it is almost always best to aim at getting everyone present into the altars to pray. Since being filled with the Spirit is an experience that must be repeated and maintained, it logically follows that every person present in the meeting needs either to be filled or re-filled with the Spirit.

More importantly, this "everyone-praying" method more fully conforms to the scriptural pattern presented in the book of Acts. Nowhere in Acts do we have the model of a few praying to be filled with the Spirit while the majority observes. The scriptural pattern is that new believers are filled with the Spirit for the first time as more seasoned disciples are being refilled with the Spirit. This model ensures that the entire church remains full of the Spirit and equipped to win the lost to Jesus. Notwithstanding, we persist in making the mistake of calling forward only those who have never been filled with the Spirit and have never before spoken in tongues. I can think of three negative results of following this flawed model:

First, when we call forward only those who have never before received the Spirit, we send the unspoken message to the congregation that one filling is enough. With our actions, we say to the people, "Since you at some time in the long distant past spoke in tongues, you don't need to pray again to be filled with the Spirit. So, just sit back, relax, and watch the show!" The truth is, however, that everyone present needs to be filled with the Spirit again and again. Thus, when we call everyone forward to be filled, we remind them that every follower of Christ needs to be continuously and repeatedly filled with the Spirit.

Second, when we call to prayer only those who have never been filled with the Spirit, we often embarrass them and make them a spectacle in front of the congregation. This situation is especially distressing to those with shy dispositions. As a result, they are discouraged from coming forward to receive the Spirit.

A third negative consequence of just calling a few to be filled with the Spirit is that the pastor often feels pressured to produce results. Because he fears failure in front of the congregation, he is tempted to neglect preaching on the subject altogether. Further, when the pastor finally does preach on the subject, in order to save face, he is tempted to manipulate or coerce the seekers into speaking in tongues, or into displaying some other physical manifestation. After all, isn't he God's man of faith and power? How will he look if the seekers are not in some way dramatically moved by his prayer? These temptations, however, can be avoided if everyone is called forward where they can ask to receive the Spirit together.

As everyone prays together, the first-time seekers can simply join in with the others to be filled with the Spirit. In this corporate context, they are more likely to be filled, since everyone's praying together creates an atmosphere permeated with the Spirit's manifest presence. Such an atmosphere serves as a great aid to those seeking to be filled or refilled with the Spirit.

3. *Offer post-prayer counsel.*[47] Conclude the altar time with post-prayer counsel. Those who have been filled with the Spirit and have spoken in tongues should be reminded that God has given them the Spirit to empower them as Christ's witnesses. Encourage them to go out and look for opportunities to share Christ with others. As they do, they can expect the Spirit of God to embolden them and anoint their words. You will also want to encourage those who have not been filled with the Spirit. Ensure them that the promise of Jesus is still true: "Everyone who asks receives."[48] Tell them to continue to seek the Spirit's empowering, knowing that, if they will do this, God will soon give them the Holy Spirit.

Review and Application

Now that you have completed this lesson, take a few moments to reflect, apply, and implement the things you have learned.

Reflect:

Reflect on the following issues:

---

[47] Since this issue of post-prayer counsel is discussed in the following chapter, "Praying with Believers to Receive the Holy Spirit," we will only briefly address it now.

[48] Luke 11:10

Chapter 7: How to Preach on the Baptism in the Holy Spirit

- Based on Acts 1:8, explain why preaching on Spirit baptism must be a priority of every Pentecostal pastor or church leader.
- List and discuss three important *goals* when preaching on the baptism in the Holy Spirit.
- Discuss the importance of *context* when preaching on Spirit baptism.
- Name and discuss three critical *elements* one should consider when preaching on the baptism in the Holy Spirit.
- List and describe the three *steps of faith* one must take to receive the Spirit.

Apply:

Based on what you have learned in this lesson, evaluate your own preaching ministry as it relates to the baptism in the Holy Spirit by asking yourself the following questions:

- How often do I preach on the baptism in the Holy Spirit? How often *should* I preach on the subject?
- When I do preach on Spirit baptism, how effective are my messages at motivating people to be filled with the Spirit? How effective are they in preparing them to be filled?
- What three things can I do now to improve my preaching and teaching on Spirit baptism?

Commit:

Finally, pray this prayer and make this commitment:

- *Prayer:* "Lord of the Harvest, fill me with the Spirit, empower me, and teach me to preach and teach more effectively on the baptism in the Holy Spirit."
- *Commitment:* "I commit myself to preach often on the baptism in the Holy Spirit and pray with believers to receive. As I do, I will faithfully apply the concepts I learned in this lesson."

Notes:

~ Chapter 8 ~

PRAYING WITH BELIEVERS TO RECEIVE THE HOLY SPIRIT

You will remember, in Chapter 2 we emphasized the importance of every follower of Christ being baptized in the Holy Spirit and empowered as His witness. This is especially true if he or she desires to be used by God in advancing His kingdom in the earth. Then, in the last chapter, we learned how one might preach more effectively on the subject of Spirit baptism. Now, in this lesson, we will take our discussion a step further. We will talk about how to lead others into this vital Christian experience. We will answer the question, "What must a minister of the gospel do once he or she has called the people to the altar to be filled with the Spirit?"

In doing this, we will present a biblically based, yet very practical model of praying with people to receive the Holy Spirit. Our Acts in Africa team members have effectively used this model in Acts 1:8 Conferences across the continent, and have witnessed hundreds being filled with the Spirit.

Preliminary Considerations

Anyone who desires to be more effective in leading seekers into the baptism in the Holy Spirit must understand three basic truths. First, he or she must understand who can be filled with the Spirit. Next, they must understand who can pray with others to be filled with the Spirit. Finally, it is necessary to know five essential qualities needed for one to receive the Holy Spirit. Let's examine these important matters.

1. Who can be filled? Anyone who has been truly born again can, and should immediately, be filled with the Holy Spirit. This empowering experience is not just for special Christians who have reached a certain level of holiness or spiritual maturity in their lives. Nor is it only for a certain class of people belonging to a particular church group or denomination. The promise is for all Christians of all ages until Jesus returns.[1] Every Christian must be filled with the Holy Spirit because every Christian is called to be a witness for Christ.[2]

2. Who can pray with others to be filled? Anyone who has himself or herself been filled with the Spirit can lead someone else into the experience. The chief requirement in praying for others to receive the Spirit is a sincere desire to see them blessed and used by God. Remember, it is not the minister's job to "get people filled with the Spirit." That's Jesus' job. He is the baptizer in the Holy Spirit.[3] The minister's job is simply to encourage people to be baptized in the Holy Spirit and give them clear instructions on how they may best respond to the Holy Spirit and be filled. He or she is to then lead them in the prayer of faith trusting God to do the work.

---

[1] Acts 2:17-18; 38-39; Ephesians 5:18
[2] John 20:21-22; Acts 1:8
[3] Luke 3:16; Acts 2:33

3. *Elements involved in receiving the Holy Spirit.* It is helpful for the preacher to understand five important spiritual elements involved in a person's being filled with the Holy Spirit. Those elements are desire, faith, prayer, obedience, and yieldedness to God. Let's look briefly at each one.

Desire. The Bible often stresses the importance of desire in seeking after God. God once said to Israel, "You will seek me and find me when you seek me with all your heart."[4] Jesus told His disciples, "Blessed are those who hunger and thirst for righteousness, for they will be filled."[5] In another place, while teaching on how to receive the Holy Spirit, Jesus said, "Seek [literally, "keep on seeking"] and you will find."[6] Persistent seeking is a fruit of desire. The candidate must know that God will give His Spirit only to those who ardently seek His face.

Faith. Faith is the prime ingredient for receiving anything from God, including the gift of the Holy Spirit. Paul reminded the Galatian Christians that they had received the Spirit, not by the works of the law, but "by hearing with faith."[7] Jesus said that the Spirit would flow through "whoever believes."[8] One aim of the person leading others into the baptism in the Holy Spirit must therefore be to inspire faith in the heart of the seeker. (We will speak more about this later in this lesson.)

Prayer. The Holy Spirit is given in answer to believing prayer. Jesus said, "Ask, and it will be given to you."[9] In another place He taught, "Whatever you ask in prayer, believe that you have received

---

[4] Jeremiah 29:13
[5] Matthew 5:6 (NIV); cf. John 7:37
[6] Luke 11:9
[7] Galatians 3:2
[8] John 7:38
[9] Luke 11:9

it, and it will be yours."[10] Jesus himself was praying when the Spirit came upon Him at His baptism.[11] Before the disciples received the Spirit at Pentecost, they "with one accord were devoting themselves to prayer."[12] Before Paul was filled with the Spirit, he spent time in prayer.[13] Anyone desiring to be filled with the Spirit must earnestly seek God's face in prayer.

Obedience. An obedient heart is another essential element in receiving the Holy Spirit. Peter said that God gives the Holy Spirit to "those who obey him."[14] He was talking specifically about those who will obey Christ's commission to share the good news with others.[15] God is ready to empower any Christian who is willing to tell others about Jesus.

Yieldedness. Just as those being baptized in water must yield themselves to the pastor, those being baptized in the Holy Spirit must yield themselves to Jesus. They should, therefore, be instructed to surrender their entire being to the Lord. This yieldedness should include spirit, mind, and body.[16] It is through such yieldedness that the Holy Spirit will fill the person, take control of their being, and begin to speak through them as the Spirit gives utterance.[17]

---

[10] Mark 11:24
[11] Luke 3:21-22
[12] Acts 1:14
[13] Acts 9:11
[14] Acts 5:32
[15] Acts 5:28-29
[16] Romans 6:13; 12:1
[17] Acts 2:4; 10:46; 19:6

The Procedure: Praying with Believers to Be Filled with the Holy Spirit

When praying with those who have responded to be filled with the Holy Spirit, it is helpful to follow a three-step model, including instruction, prayer engagement, and post-prayer guidance.[18]

Step 1: Instruction

Clear instructions must be given either at the end of the sermon, before you call the seekers to the front, or after the seekers come forward. During this time, you will want to accomplish two objectives. First, you will want to affirm and inspire the candidates' faith. Then, you will need to clearly explain to them what they must do to be filled with the Spirit.

1. Affirmation and inspiration. Once the seekers have gathered in the front, you will want to affirm them by saying, "I am so glad you came forward to receive the Spirit. You did the right thing, and God is pleased." You could also say, "This could be one of the greatest days of your life. God has a very special gift for you." Remember, the candidates are probably nervous at this point. These words will help set them at ease and prepare their hearts to receive the Holy Spirit.

2. Explanation. The explanation will take a bit longer. In this part of the instruction process, as mentioned in the last lesson, you will have three primary goals: to stir up expectant faith in the hearts of the candidates, to bring them to a more accurate understanding of what

---

[18] This procedure is to be used in praying for a group of people who have responded *en masse* to be filled with the Spirit. For instructions on praying with individuals to receive the Holy Spirit in more private settings, see the author's book, *Power Encounter: Ministering in the Power and Anointing of the Holy Spirit,* Chapter 2, "How to Pray with Believers to Be Filled with the Holy Spirit" (Springfield, MO: PneumaLife Publications, 2013), 135-146.

they must do to receive the Spirit, and to let them know what they can expect to happen when God fills them.

One way to encourage their faith is to remind the seekers of God's promises concerning the Holy Spirit. Assure them that, if they are committed to do God's will, Jesus is committed to filling them with the Holy Spirit. Remind them of His promise: "Ask and it will be given to you… everyone who asks receives."[19] The seekers must believe that God will, the moment they ask, fill them with His Spirit. This is what we call "expectant faith." The seekers should therefore expect to be filled with the Spirit, and to speak with other tongues as the Spirit gives them utterance. Further, they should be prepared to act on that expectation.

Next, you will explain to the candidates exactly what they must do to be filled with the Spirit, and what they can expect to happen as they are being filled. They need to know that receiving the Holy Spirit is not a difficult nor extraordinary thing for a believer. It is, in fact, the normal thing for a Christian to do. They should know that they will not be filled with "another Holy Spirit" but the same Holy Spirit who has indwelt them since the day they first received Christ as Savior.

You can tell the seekers, "Receiving the Holy Spirit is easy! It is the natural thing to do. In fact, for the born again Christian, it is as easy as breathing." And it's true! Remember what Jesus did with His disciples: "He breathed on [or into] them and said, 'Receive the Holy Spirit.'"[20] Receiving the Holy Spirit is much like breathing. Just as breathing is the natural thing for a person to do, receiving the Holy Spirit is the natural thing for the child of God to do.

Next, let the candidates know exactly what you plan to do and what will happen to them. You could say something like this:

---

[19] Luke 11:9-10
[20] John 20:22

"I will lead you in three steps of faith. *First, we will ask in faith.* By this, I mean that we will simply and sincerely ask God to give us His Spirit. As we do, we will believe that He is hearing and answering our prayer. We will then open our hearts to God and sense His Spirit coming upon us. Once we sense the Spirit's presence, we will take our second step of faith.

"We will receive by faith. I will lead you in a second prayer. It will go something like this, 'I now invite the Holy Spirit to come inside me and fill me. By faith, right now, in Jesus' name, I receive the Holy Spirit.' We will then 'believe that we have received.'[21] The instant we believe, the Holy Spirit will fill us, and we will sense His powerful Presence deep within—in our innermost beings. We will then take our third step of faith.

"We will begin to speak in faith. We will speak as the Spirit gives utterance. The words will not come from our minds, as in normal speech, but from our spirits where we sense the Presence of God inside. As we speak, we will begin to say words we do not understand. When this happens, don't be afraid. Continue to speak in faith knowing that God is graciously filling you with His Holy Spirit!"

Then ask, "Do you have any questions? Are you ready to be filled with the Spirit?" If the seekers have questions, answer them. If they have no questions, proceed to the prayer engagement.

Step 2: Prayer Engagement

In the prayer engagement, you will lead the candidates in their three steps of faith just described. They will ask in faith, receive by faith, and speak in faith. As you pray with the seekers, become a seeker yourself, allowing God to refill you with the Holy Spirit.

1. Lead the seekers to ask in faith. Much as you would lead a sinner in the sinner's prayer, you now lead the seekers in a prayer

---

[21] Mark 11:24

asking God to fill them with the Spirit. The prayer may proceed as follows, with the candidates repeating each line:

> "Lord, I come now to be filled with the Holy Spirit. / You promised that I would receive power when I received the Spirit. / I need that power to be your witness. / Right now, there is nothing I want more. / You have promised that everyone who asks, receives. / I am asking; therefore, I expect to receive. / When I begin to speak, I will release my faith. / I will not be afraid. / I will begin to pray in tongues as Your Spirit gives me utterance. / Come Holy Spirit and fill me now."

After you have prayed, assure the candidates that God has heard their prayer, and that He is ready now to fill them with the Spirit. Encourage them to be spiritually sensitive to the presence of the Spirit who has come to fill them. You may want to take a few moments to quietly worship the Lord together, responding to His presence.

2. Help the seekers receive by faith. You may now ask the seekers to lift their hands toward heaven and pray this simple prayer of faith with you. "Lord, right now, in Jesus Name, I receive the Holy Spirit. Holy Spirit, come inside me and fill me. According to Jesus' promise, I believe that I have received." This prayer provides a definite point in time where the seekers can focus their faith to receive the Holy Spirit. They should, at that moment, truly *believe that they have received.* The moment each one believes, the Spirit will come and fill them. Encourage them to be aware of the Spirit's coming into their spirits. They will sense the Spirit's presence deep inside.

3. Encourage the seekers to speak by faith. Tell them that, once they sense the Spirit's Presence within, they should act in bold faith and allow Him to flow through them. They should cooperate fully with what the Spirit is doing by yielding their vocal organs and lips to Him, trusting Him to give them the words. They will begin to speak words in a language they have never learned. The words will come from deep within, from where they sense the Spirit's moving inside.

Tell them not to be fearful, but to cooperate fully with the Spirit by continuing to speak in faith.

If some do not immediately begin to speak in tongues, encourage them to continue yielding themselves to the Lord. If they still have difficulty responding, you may want to repeat the above procedure. As you do, point out how they may more perfectly respond in faith to the Spirit. Once they begin to speak in tongues, encourage them to continue. Remain with them in prayer as long as they continue to pray in the Spirit.

Step 3: Post-prayer Guidance

As mentioned in the last lesson, it is important that post-prayer guidance be given to the candidates. To those who have been filled, you will give one kind of counsel; to those who have not been filled, you will give another.

1. Those who are filled with the Spirit. For those candidates who are filled with the Spirit and speak in tongues, the following advice is appropriate. Tell them that receiving the Spirit is not an end in itself; it is a means to a greater end. The primary purpose for receiving the Spirit is that we may receive power for witness. Remember Jesus' words: "You will receive power when the Holy Spirit has come upon you, and you will be my witnesses…"[22]

You may want to say, "This is just the beginning. God will now begin to use you in new and powerful ways. Expect to have new power in your life. Go out right now and tell someone about Jesus." You will want to add, "You should also spend time each day praying in the Spirit (that is, in tongues). This will give you boldness and strength and will remind you of the Spirit's empowering presence in your life."

---

[22] Acts 1:8

2. Those who are not filled with the Spirit. If some are not filled with the Spirit, you will want to give the following encouragement and advice. Tell them not to be discouraged because they did not receive the Holy Spirit at this time. Assure them that the promise of Jesus is still true: "Everyone who asks receives."[23] Tell them that they should keep asking and they will receive, keep seeking and they will find, and keep knocking and the door will be opened unto them.[24] You may want to pray again, encouraging the seekers to act in bold faith.

Other Important Considerations

As we conclude this lesson, let's look at three other issues worthy of consideration when leading others into the baptism in the Holy Spirit:

1. Know what the Bible says. First, if one is going to help others be filled with the Spirit, it makes sense that he or she should seek to know all they can on the subject. Most importantly, they should study the Word of God, especially the book of Acts, to see what it says. Further, they could read and study good books on the subject.[25] The more one knows about the Holy Spirit and His work in the lives of people, the better able they will be to help others experience His power.

2. Don't be lazy. If you would help God's people receive the Holy Spirit, don't let spiritual laziness disqualify you. Because it is often hard work to pray with people to be filled with the Spirit, some shy away from preaching on the subject and seeking to lead others into the experience. If that is the case with you, repent of your spiritual laziness, and give yourself wholeheartedly to this vital ministry.

---

[23] Luke 11:10

[24] Literal paraphrase of Luke 11:9

[25] You can find a list of such books at the end of this book.

3. *Watch your intensity level.* When praying with others to be filled with the Spirit, it is important that you watch your intensity level. By this I mean you should be upbeat and positive when praying with them. Let your enthusiasm show! At the same time, you should beware of being too pushy. Wisdom will show you the right balance between intensity and reserve in encouraging people to be filled with the Spirit.

In this lesson, we have talked about how you can be effective in leading people into the baptism in the Holy Spirit. We hope that you will now dedicate yourself to the task. There is nothing more satisfying than helping others personally experience the Spirit's power and presence in their lives.

Review and Application

In mobilizing the church for missions, both Jesus and the apostles emphasized the necessity of disciples being empowered by the Holy Spirit. Any pastor or church leader wanting to lead their church into effective evangelistic outreach and church planting must do the same.

Reflect:

Having completed this lesson, reflect on the following issues:

- List and explain the five important spiritual elements involved in a person's being filled with the Holy Spirit.
- When leading believers to receive the Spirit, discuss two objectives you want to accomplish during the time of instruction.
- Discuss how you can lead seekers into each of their three steps of faith in receiving the Holy Spirit.

Apply:

Now, make the following applications to your present ministry:

- Evaluate your own effectiveness in leading believers into the baptism in the Holy Spirit.

- Make a list of those things you can do to better prepare yourself to lead others into Spirit baptism.
- Plan to preach on the baptism in the Holy Spirit soon. When you do, apply the lessons you have learned in this and the last chapter.

Commit:

In closing, pray this prayer and make this commitment:

- *Prayer:* "Lord Jesus, send Your Spirit upon me. Anoint me and fill me with a passion to see God's people baptized in the Holy Spirit. And teach me how to lead them into this vital Christian experience."
- *Commitment:* "I commit to do whatever is necessary to learn how to effectively lead people into the baptism in the Holy Spirit."

~ Chapter 9 ~

Pentecost and the Next Generation[1]

The moment the baton is passed from one runner to the next is a critical time in a relay race. How well this task is performed can affect the outcome of the race. If the baton is passed smoothly, momentum is maintained, and the team increases its chance of winning. However, if the handoff is bungled, or the baton is dropped, momentum is lost, along with any chance of winning the race.

This lesson is about passing the baton of Pentecost from one generation to the next. If the baton is passed smoothly, the revival will continue and the mission will prosper. If the transfer is bungled, the revival will wane and the mission will stall. Educational reformer, John Dewey, once said, if democracy is to survive, it "must be reborn

---

[1] This lesson was originally developed by AIA team member, Mark Turney. Most of what is said here are his thoughts on the subject.

each generation."[2] The same can be said of authentic Pentecostalism. If it is to survive in Africa (or anywhere else), it must be reborn in the heart of every generation. If we fail to pass the baton of authentic (think biblical, missional) Pentecostalism to the next generation, the movement will inevitably mutate into a mere characterization of what is so clearly presented in the book of Acts.

In this lesson, we will remind ourselves of our responsibility to pass Pentecost to the next generation. But before we look at this responsibility, let's first review some of the promises in Scripture concerning how the gift of the Spirit is available to all—including our young people and children.

A Promise for All

Scripture teaches that the promise of Pentecost is for all God's people. It is for men and women, rich and poor, young and old. On the Day of Pentecost, God poured out His Spirit on the waiting disciples. Luke describes the event like this:

> "When the day of Pentecost arrived, they were *all* together in one place. And suddenly there came from heaven a sound like a mighty rushing wind, and it filled the entire house where they were sitting. And divided tongues as of fire appeared to them and rested on *each one* of them. And they were *all* filled with the Holy Spirit and began to speak in other tongues as the Spirit gave them utterance."[3]

Note how the Bible emphasizes that at Pentecost "all" and "each one" was filled with the Spirit. Peter then stood, and quoting from the prophet Joel, explained to the gathered crowd the significance of what they had just observed. "This is what was uttered through the prophet Joel," he declared, "'And in the last days it shall be, God declares,

---

[2] John Dewey, *Democracy and Education* (New York: Macmillan, 1916).

[3] Acts 2:1-4 (emphasis added)

that I will pour out my Spirit on all flesh, and *your sons and your daughters* shall prophesy…and *your young men* shall see visions, and your old men shall dream dreams…"[4] The promise of the Spirit thus includes old and young alike.

In concluding His sermon, Peter returned to this inclusivity theme. He instructed the people,

> "Repent and be baptized *every one of you* in the name of Jesus Christ for the forgiveness of your sins, and you will receive the gift of the Holy Spirit. For the promise is for you and *for your children* and for *all* who are far off, *everyone* whom the Lord our God calls to himself."[5]

Again, the promise of the Spirit is "for all…for everyone God calls to himself." Peter adds that it is even for "your children." God wants every adult, young person, and child to receive the gift of the Holy Spirit.

Once the disciples tried to prevent some children from coming to the Lord. When Jesus saw this, He rebuked them, saying, "Let the children come to me, and do not hinder them, for to such belongs the kingdom of God."[6] Jesus wants to receive and bless our children. We, nevertheless, tell them, "When you become an adult, you can come to God." But Jesus tells us, "When you become like a child, I will receive you."

The kingdom of God belongs to those with childlike faith. It follows, therefore, that children can experience all the blessings of the kingdom—including Spirit baptism. Surely, the Father will not withhold the promised gift of the Spirit from them.[7] We should therefore teach our young people and children about the baptism in the Holy Spirit, and we should pray with them to receive the Spirit.

---

[4] Acts 2:17 (emphasis added); cf. Joel 2:28
[5] Acts 2:38-39 (emphasis added)
[6] Luke 18:16-17
[7] Luke 11:13; Acts 1:4; 2:38-39

Chapter 9: Pentecost and the Next Generation

The story is told of D. L. Moody, the nineteenth-century American evangelist. It illustrates the value of children to the kingdom of God. Moody once told a colleague, "In the service last evening, two and one half people were saved." His colleague replied, "I think I know what you mean. You mean two adults and one child were saved." Smiling, Moody answered, "No. I mean two children and one adult were saved, because the adult has already lived half his life for the devil, but the children have their whole lives to serve God." The same applies to Spirit-baptism. When a child or young person is empowered by the Spirit, it opens to them a lifetime of effective witness and Christian service.

The angel's prophecy concerning John the Baptist supports this truth. The angel announced to Zachariah, John's father, "He will be filled with the Holy Spirit, even from his mother's womb," or as one translation puts it, "while yet in his mother's womb."[8] Later, when John's mother, Elizabeth, was pregnant, Mary the mother of Jesus came to visit her. The moment she saw Mary, "the baby [John] leaped in her womb. And Elizabeth was filled with the Holy Spirit."[9] At that moment, both the mother and the yet-to-be-born child were filled with the Spirit.

While John's experience is unique, it nevertheless demonstrates that no child is too young to receive God's Spirit. We should therefore encourage our children to be filled with the Spirit, even at a very young age. In our travels across Africa, our Acts in Africa team has seen many children filled with the Spirit and speak in tongues as the Spirit flowed through them.[10] Children need to be filled with the Spirit for the same reason their parents need to be filled, so they can more effectively tell their friends about Jesus.

---

[8] Luke 1:15 (NIV, New American Standard Bible)

[9] Luke 1:41, cf. 44

[10] You can find resources for teaching children about the Holy Spirit at www.DecadeofPentecost.org/childrens-ministry/.

A Responsibility to Shoulder

Christ requires of us that we pass Pentecost to succeeding generations. We must not fail in this awesome responsibility. Both Scripture and history teach us that, if not adequately emphasized, this biblical truth, along with its accompanying experience, will be lost.

This fact is illustrated in the story of Eli. Though he himself was a godly man, he did not pass on his faith to his sons. As result, they became "worthless men" who "did not know the Lord." Their brazen disregard for the law of God brought disgrace and defeat on the family of Eli, and ultimately on all the people of God. Because of this failure, God judged Eli and his household.[11] We must not make the same mistake with our children. If not carefully passed to the next generation, the baton of God's promise can be dropped and the truth of Spirit baptism lost.

Another example of this negative pattern is the experience of the church in North Africa and Europe. Because God's truth was not passed from one generation to the next, Christianity in these places became insipid, like salt that had lost its saltiness.[12] The churches had an appearance of godliness, yet they denied God's power."[13] Eventually, the church in North Africa was overwhelmed by Islam, and the church in Europe succumbed to secular humanism. The same could easily happen with our Pentecostal heritage in Africa. If not carefully passed on to our children, the dream of a last-days Spirit-empowered missions force from Africa's soil could fall to the ground and die. This would be a tragedy of epic proportions.

After receiving the Law from God, Moses emphasized the importance of passing the truth it contained to succeeding generations. He cautioned Israel, "Take care, and keep your soul

---

[11] 1 Samuel 2:12-36; 3:1-4:22
[12] Matthew 5:13
[13] 2 Timothy 3:5

diligently, lest you forget the things that your eyes have seen, and lest they depart from your heart all the days of your life." He then added, "Make them known to your children and your children's children."[14] The writer of Hebrews issued a similar exhortation to the Jewish Christians of his day: "Therefore we must pay much closer attention to what we have heard, lest we drift away from it."[15] The same applies to us today. What we have received from God, we must pass to our children.

This then begs the question, how can we who have experienced the power of the Spirit in our own lives pass the experience to seceding generations? We can do this several ways. Let's look at three of those ways:

1. Personally experience the Spirit. Before we can pass authentic Pentecostalism to the next generation, we must allow the Spirit to work mightily in our own lives. How can we give to another what we do not possess ourselves? When Peter healed the lame man at the Beautiful Gate, he told him, "What I have I give to you."[16] Peter could say this because he had something to give. He had received the Spirit at Pentecost,[17] and because he had submitted himself to Christ's authority, he could speak to the man in Jesus' name.[18]

Before we can pass Pentecost to the next generation, we too must have genuinely experienced the power of Pentecost. In other words, we must ensure that we have truly been born of and baptized in the Holy Spirit,[19] and that we are striving to live "in step with the

---

[14] Deuteronomy 4:9
[15] Hebrews 2:1
[16] Acts 3:6
[17] Acts 2:4
[18] John 14:13-14. To minister in Christ's name is to submit to His authority and to do what He has commanded (Luke 7:8).
[19] John 3:5-6; Acts 1:4-5

Spirit."[20] Our children and youth must see how our walk with the Spirit has affected our lives. The fruit and gifts of the Spirit should be evident.[21] As our children observe how the Spirit has shaped our lives, they will want the same in theirs.

2. Start in the home. The home is the most effective place to train our children. We must therefore teach Christian parents how to nurture their children in the ways of the Lord. Moses spoke of this parental responsibility. He admonished them,

> "Now this is the commandment, the statutes and the rules that the Lord your God commanded me to teach you, that you may do them in the land to which you are going over, to possess it, that you may fear the Lord your God, you and your son and your son's son, by keeping all his statutes and his commandments, which I command you.... You shall teach them diligently to your children, and shall talk of them when you sit in your house, and when you walk by the way, and when you lie down, and when you rise."[22]

If we are serious about passing authentic Pentecostalism to our children, we must begin in our Pentecostal homes.

3. Train in the church. Training that begins in the home should continue in the church. To pass Pentecost to the next generation we must very intentionally and deliberately teach our children about the Father's promise to give the Holy Spirit to His children.[23] We must further pray with them and give them many opportunities to be filled with the Spirit.

---

[20] Galatians 5:16, 25 (NIV)
[21] Galatians 5:22-23; 1 Corinthians 12:8-10
[22] Deuteronomy 6:1-2, 7
[23] Luke 11:13; Acts 2:38-39

A Warning to Heed

A warning is in order here. Authentic Pentecostalism is always just one generation away from extinction. If we fail to pass Pentecost to the next generation, our churches will die spiritually and the advance of God's mission will be slowed. Naturalists speak of certain "endangered species" in Africa. Among those vulnerable animals are Africa's "Big Five," including the African elephant, the lion, the Cape buffalo, the rhinoceros, and the leopard. If measures are not taken to protect these species, they, along with several others, could become extinct. The same is true of authentic Pentecostalism. If we fail to take the necessary measures to pass Pentecost to succeeding generations, the "Pentecostal species" could become extinct.

We must therefore be very intentional about leading our youth and children into the baptism in the Holy Spirit. This truth is illustrated in the story of the Judges. The Bible tells us,

> "There arose another generation after them who did not know the Lord or the work that he had done for Israel. And the people of Israel did what was evil in the sight of the Lord.... And they abandoned the Lord, the God of their fathers, who had brought them out of the land of Egypt. They went after other gods..."[24]

How foolish and shortsighted we would be to assume that, just because children and young people are in church today, this alone will cause them to grow up and serve the Lord faithfully. If we want to see the next generation involved in God's mission, we must ensure that they have committed themselves to that mission and that they personally experience the power of the Holy Spirit.

---

[24] Judges 2:10-12

A Plan to Follow

What then must we do to ensure that we successfully pass Pentecost to the next generation? Summing up what we have already mentioned in this lesson, we recommend the following:

- We must diligently teach our children and young people about God's mission and their role in fulfilling that mission.
- We must teach them about the Holy Spirit and how He will empower them to participate in God's mission.
- We must offer frequent opportunities for our children and young people to receive the Holy Spirit.
- We must pray for them, and with them, to receive the Spirit, and we must show them how to live daily in the Spirit's power and presence.
- As pastors, we must train parents to lead their children into the Spirit-empowered life.

In the 2008 Olympic Games in Beijing, China, both the American men's and the American women's 400 meter relay teams were favored to win gold medals.[25] They had the fastest runners and the most experienced teams. Yet, in the semifinals, tragedy struck causing both teams to leave Beijing empty-handed.

In the men's race, things went well for the US team through the first two legs. However, when Gary Patton closed in on Tyson Gay for the second handoff, something went wrong. Patton lunged forward to hand the stick to Gay. However, when Gay's hand closed, nothing was there. The crowd gasped in disbelief as the baton fell to the ground and bounced off the rain-slickened track. The men lost the race and were eliminated from the competition.

---

[25] Https://www.foxnews.com/story/dropped-batons-cost-u-s-mens-womens-relay-teams. Accessed November 20, 2008.

The American women were also in the lead heading into the final exchange. However, just as with the men, something went amiss. Torri Edwards failed to pass the baton to anchor Lauryn Williams. As the stick fell to the ground, Edwards shrieked and covered her face with her hands. Williams went back to retrieve the stick, and she heroically finished the race—but the Americans were dead last.

For the men's relay team, it was the first time the Americans failed to reach the Olympic finals since 1912. For the women's team it was the first time since 1948. Both teams had the talent and speed. Yet both lost because they failed to make a good handoff.

The same can happen to the Pentecostal movement in Africa. If we fail to effectively pass the baton of authentic missional Pentecostalism to our youth and children, all our gains will be lost. However, if we are successful in the effort, Africa's missionary future will be bright.

Review and Application

Now that you have completed this lesson, take a few moments to reflect, apply, and implement what you have learned.

Reflect:

Reflect on the following issues:

- According to Acts 2:16-17 (cf. Joel 2:28) to whom is the gift of the Spirit promised?
- Based on what you have learned in this lesson, describe our responsibility as Pentecostal parents and leaders concerning the children and youth of our churches.

Apply:

Now, make the following applications to your present ministry:

- Evaluate your church or ministry as to how effective you have been in passing the baton of Pentecost to the next generation.

- Develop a strategy defining how your church will fulfill its responsibility of ensuring that the youth and children have been empowered by the Spirit and mobilized as witnesses to their friends and schools.

Commit:

In closing, pray this prayer and make this commitment:

- *Prayer:* "Lord of the Harvest, give us the will and the wisdom we need to pass the baton of authentic missional Pentecostalism to our children."

- *Commitment:* "Jesus, we commit ourselves to do whatever is necessary to ensure that our children and youth know Jesus, and that they have been baptized in the Holy Spirit and empowered to reach their generation for Christ."

Chapter 9: Pentecost and the Next Generation

Notes:

~ Chapter 10 ~

WOMEN AND PENTECOSTAL REVIVAL[1]

In his Pentecost sermon, Peter announced that God had opened the way for women to become fully-qualified and fully-authorized participants in His mission. The apostle declared,

> "This is what was uttered through the prophet Joel: 'And in the last days it shall be, God declares, that I will pour out my Spirit on all flesh, and your sons and *your daughters shall prophesy*...even on my male servants and *female servants* in those days I will pour out my Spirit, and they shall prophesy.'"[2]

Because God would empower them by His Spirit, in this new Age of the Spirit, women would be qualified to speak on God's behalf just

---

[1] This message was originally developed by Acts in Africa team member, Sandy Miller.

[2] Acts 2:16-18; cf. Joel 2:28-29

as the men. In this lesson, we will examine the role of Pentecostal women in advancing God's mission in the power of the Holy Spirit.

The Bible Guides Us

As "people of the Book," we begin our discussion of women in ministry with God's Word. In the Bible, we discover that throughout sacred history God has called and used women to actively participate in His mission. The Old Testament speaks of several of those women. In Judges, God used a woman named Deborah as a prophet and a judge.[3] As a prophet, she spoke on God's behalf and called Israel to turn from their idolatry back to the true and living God. As a judge, she counselled the people and helped them make wise choices. God further anointed her to lead God's people into battle to defeat the Canaanite army of Sisera.[4]

Huldah was another prophet used by God.[5] She was an advisor to Josiah, king of Judah, and his court. By the power of the Spirit, this woman of God boldly prophesied that God would judge Judah because of their idolatry. Her prophecy prompted the king to repent.[6] According to Jewish tradition, Deborah and Huldah were two of the "seven prophetesses of Israel," with Sarah, Miriam, Hannah, Abigail, and Esther.

God also called, anointed, and used women in the New Testament. Luke has much to say about this. In his gospel, he tells how the Holy Spirit came on the virgin, Mary, causing her to conceive the Christ child.[7] Soon after that, she visited her elder cousin, Elizabeth, and prophesied over her.[8] Elizabeth, who was

---

[3] Judges 4:4-5
[4] Judges 4:6-15
[5] 2 Kings 22:14-20; 2 Chronicles 34:22-28
[6] 2 Kings 22:15-17
[7] Luke 1:35-38
[8] Luke 1:46-56. This prophecy is sometimes called "The Magnificat."

pregnant with John, was then filled with the Holy Spirit, and she also spoke prophetically.[9] Later, Luke tells us that an elderly prophetess named Anna met Mary and Joseph with the infant Jesus in the temple and prophesied over him.[10]

In Acts, Luke further demonstrates how God wants to use women to advance His kingdom in the earth. Before returning to heaven, Jesus commanded His disciples to wait in Jerusalem until they had been baptized in the Holy Spirit. He told them that, when this happened, they would receive power to be His witnesses "in Jerusalem and in all Judea and Samaria, and to the end of the earth."[11]

We know Jesus' promise included the women because they gathered with the men to pray and be filled with the Spirit.[12] Then, when God poured out His Spirit on the Day of Pentecost, "they were *all* filled with the Holy Spirit and began to speak in other tongues as the Spirit gave them utterance."[13] The "all" in this case includes both the men and women. Thus, at Pentecost the women...

- ...obeyed the *same command* as the men: "[Jesus] ordered them not to depart from Jerusalem, but to wait for the promise of the Father, which, he said, 'you heard from me, for John baptized with water, but you will be baptized with the Holy Spirit not many days from now.'"
- ...received the *same promise* as the men: "But you will receive power when the Holy Spirit has come upon you...."
- ...waited for the *same purpose* as the men: "...and you will be my witnesses in Jerusalem and in all Judea and Samaria, and to the end of the earth."

---

[9] Luke 1:39-45
[10] Luke 2:36-38
[11] Acts 1:4-5, 8
[12] Acts 1:14
[13] Acts 2:4 (emphasis added)

- ...had the *same experience* as the men: "They were all filled with the Holy Spirit..."
- ...manifested the *same missional sign* as the men: "And [they all] began to speak in other tongues as the Spirit gave them utterance."

In other words, God the Holy Spirit calls and empowers women for the same purpose He calls and empowers men—to be Christ's Spirit-empowered witnesses at home and to the ends of the earth. What qualifies individuals (both men and women) for ministry is not their gender but the calling of Christ and the empowering of the Spirit.

This truth is further emphasized in Peter's Pentecost sermon. After the Spirit was poured out at Pentecost, Peter stood and explained to the people what had happened:

> "This is what was uttered through the prophet Joel, 'In the last days it shall be,' God declares, 'that I will pour out my Spirit on *all flesh,* and your sons *and your daughters* shall prophesy, and your young men shall see visions, and your old men shall dream dreams; even on my male servants *and female servants* in those days I will pour out my Spirit, and they [all my servants both men and women] shall prophesy.'"[14]

Here, Peter states a universal principle for the Age of the Spirit. God will anoint all of His people to be His Spirit-empowered witnesses regardless of age, gender, or social standing.

Paul affirmed the same when he wrote, "There is neither Jew nor Greek, there is neither slave nor free, there is no male and female, for you are all one in Christ Jesus."[15] In his first letter to the Christians in Corinth, Paul encouraged women to pray publically and to prophesy

---

[14] Acts 2:16-18 (emphasis added)
[15] Galatians 3:28

in the church so long as their heads were covered according to local custom.[16]

In the closing chapter of Romans, the apostle commended Junia, saying she was "outstanding among the apostles."[17] He also sent greetings to Priscilla and Aquila, calling them "fellow workers in Christ Jesus."[18] This wife-husband ministry team often ministered alongside Paul.[19] Together, they mentored the mighty preacher, Apollos and "explained to him the way of God more accurately."[20]

On two occasions, Paul limited the speech of women in the church.[21] However, in light of the above, we are to understand that he was dealing with parochial issues in local congregations. Two other indications in the New Testament that women should be involved in ministry are the fact that Christ chose women to be the first witnesses announcing the good news of His resurrection[22] and Philip's four daughters who prophesied.[23]

Our Heritage Inspires Us

Not only does Scripture charge women to participate in God's mission, our Pentecostal heritage inspires them to do the same. From the beginning, Pentecostal churches have encouraged women to be filled with the Spirit and freely proclaim the good news to all.

Many scholars trace the beginning of the modern Pentecostal Movement to an outpouring of the Spirit on January 1, 1901, at the Bethel Bible Training School in Topeka, Kansas, USA. There, a

---

[16] 1 Corinthians 11:5
[17] Romans 16:7 (NIV)
[18] Romans 16:3
[19] Acts 18:2, 18; 1 Corinthians 16:19; 2 Timothy 4:19
[20] Acts 18:24-26
[21] 1 Corinthians 14:34-35; 1 Timothy 2:11-15
[22] Mark 16:9-11; John 20:18
[23] Acts 21:8

group of gospel workers assembled to study God's word and to seek His face. During an all-night prayer meeting, the Spirit fell upon and filled several of the students. Amazingly, they began to speak in tongues, just as the 120 did on the Day of Pentecost.[24]

It is not without significance that the first person to receive the Spirit was a humble woman named Agnes Ozman. As in the book of Acts, where a woman named Lydia became the first person to receive the gospel in Europe,[25] in Topeka, a woman named Agnes became the first person to receive the Spirit in the modern Pentecostal revival. In 1917, she received ministerial credentials from the newly-formed Assemblies of God.

Five years after the Topeka outpouring, God poured out His Spirit again in Los Angeles, California, at the famous Azusa Street Mission. During this revival, many women of various ethnic backgrounds were filled with the Spirit and enabled to preach with power. God used some of them to plant Pentecostal churches throughout the USA and in other parts of the world. Along with the men, gifted women gave spiritual and administrative oversight to the work. In fact, six of the twelve administrative elders at the Azusa Street mission were women. As such, they were entrusted with the duty of ordaining evangelists, planting churches, and sending out missionaries from the mission.

These Pentecostal women believed that the Spirit himself had qualified them to preach the gospel. They based this belief on Jesus' promise of Acts 1:8 and on Joel's promise in 2:28-29, which Peter quoted on the Day of Pentecost. Two notable women were Lucy Farrow and Julia Hutchins. These African American women went from Azusa to Liberia as early Pentecostal missionaries. Today, more than half of Assemblies of God (USA) foreign missionaries are women. Across Africa, Spirit-filled women are taking the lead as never before.

---

[24] Acts 2:4
[25] Acts 16:14

The Need of the Hour Moves Us

Not only does Scripture and our Pentecostal heritage demand that we allow women to fully participate in proclaiming the good news, the need of the hour compels us to do the same. The Africa Assemblies of God are involved in a great Decade of Pentecost stretching from Pentecost Sunday 2010 to Pentecost Sunday 2020.[26] They have set a collective goal of seeing 10 million new believers baptized in the Holy Spirit and empowered as witnesses, church planters, and cross-cultural missionaries. In Acts 1:8 Conferences held across the continent, they have committed themselves to plant more than 49,000 new Spirit-empowered missionary churches—many among the more than 850 unreached people groups in Sub-Saharan Africa. In addition, Africa AG church leaders are looking beyond 2020 to an even greater harvest in the following decade. All of this is being done in realization that Jesus could return at any moment.[27]

To accomplish these ambitious goals, everyone is needed. Jesus once told His disciples, "The harvest is plentiful, but the laborers are few."[28] How unwise (and unbiblical) we would be to marginalized more than half our work force during this critical time. In Africa, during the time of harvest, every able-bodied person goes to the fields to reap the grain—men, women, and children. No one is excluded, because the stakes are too high. Rogue animals could pillage the grain, thieves could steal it, or inclement weather could destroy it. Jesus said, "When the grain is ripe, at once [the farmer] puts in the sickle, because the harvest has come."[29] During this time of extraordinary opportunity, everyone is needed in God's harvest field, and women are ready to do their part.

---

[26] Website: www.DecadeofPentecost.org
[27] Matthew 24:27, 44
[28] Matthew 9:37
[29] Mark 4:29

Jesus challenges us, "Open your eyes and look at the fields! They are ripe for harvest."[30] We must lift up our eyes and see Africa as Jesus sees it. Across the continent, millions of lost people dwell in thousands of unreached places. Today, the church has more opportunities than it does workers. Therefore, we must not hesitate to mobilize Africa's Spirit-filled women to help reap this great harvest of souls before it is eternally too late. The words of the psalmist will then come to pass: "The Lord gives the word; the women who announce the news are a great host."[31]

Women's Unique Gifts Compel Us

God has given women certain gifts that can be used to advance His kingdom. These unique abilities commend them to participate in the mission of God. They further compel the church to employ them. For instance, overall women are more determined, more compassionate, and more sensitive to the needs of people and to the voice of God than are men. While men also possess these qualities, women seem to possess them in greater measure. Give a woman a job, and she will persevere until it is finished.

Women also have an exceptional ability to look into people's hearts and to identify with their pain. Some women possess an openness to the voice of the Spirit and an ability to hear the voice of the Spirit that few men possess. These qualities compel the church to open the door of ministry to women.

In addition to having unique gifts, women have unique opportunities to share the message of Christ with others. Women can readily go places and do things that men cannot do. For instance, women can talk to other women about sensitive issues. This is especially true when it comes to sharing the good news with Muslim women. While a man would never be able to share the gospel with a married Islamic

---

[30] John 4:35 (NIV)
[31] Psalm 68:11

woman, the door stands wide open for women. Such opportunities demand a response. Our Spirit-filled women must be allowed to fully participate in ministry to the lost and to the body of Christ.

What We Must Do Now

What can you, as a Pentecostal woman, do to prepare yourself to effectively participate in God's mission? Allow me to suggest three things:

1. Gain understanding. To successfully participate in advancing God's mission in the earth, one must have a clear understanding of what that mission is. We discussed this in Chapter 1, where we said that God's mission is His purpose and work in the world in relation to fallen humanity. God's mission is to redeem and call unto himself a people out of every kindred, tongue, and nation on earth.[32]

In this context, each Pentecostal woman must seek to understand her unique role in fulfilling that mission. This understanding can only be gained through an intimate relationship with God, and through diligent study of His Word. A good place to begin is to carefully study the lessons taught in this book, and to diligently apply them to your life.[33]

2. Experience the Spirit. Further, if you sincerely want to be used by God to effectively participate in His mission, you will need a genuine experience with the Holy Spirit. Only then will you be able to fully discern God's plan as revealed in His word. And only then will you be able to discern God's voice as He speaks by His Spirit to your spirit.

---

[32] Revelation 5:9; cf. Matthew 24:14

[33] Other helpful books can be downloaded for free from the www.DecadeofPentecost.org website. Especially pertinent to our discussion is Mark R. Turney's book, *Encountering God's Missionary Spirit.*

Any woman wanting to be used by God must have two essential spiritual experiences. First, she must be born of the Spirit.[34] Then, she must be empowered by the Spirit.[35] One is born of the Spirit when he or she is saved, as were the people of Samaria when they "believed Philip as he preached the good news."[36] One is empowered by the Spirit when he or she is filled with the Holy Spirit, as were the Samaritans when Peter and John laid hands on them "and they received the Holy Spirit."[37] To be saved one must repent of their sins and put their faith in Christ alone for salvation.[38] To be filled with the Spirit, as were the women on the Day of Pentecost, one must take Christ at His promise and confidently approach God's throne in prayer.[39] To receive the Spirit now, simply take these three "steps of faith":

- *Ask in faith:* Jesus promised, "Ask, and it will be given to you....the heavenly Father [will] give the Holy Spirit to those who ask him!"[40]
- *Receive by faith:* Jesus further promised, "Everyone who asks receives..."[41] He said, "Whatever you ask in prayer, *believe that you have received* it, and it will be yours."[42]
- *Speak in faith:* When the disciples received the Spirit on the Day of Pentecost, they *"began to speak* in other tongues as the Spirit gave them utterance."[43] You can expect to do the same when you are filled with the Spirit.

---

[34] John 3:3-7
[35] Acts 1:8; 2:4
[36] Acts 8:12
[37] Acts 8:17
[38] Mark 1:15; Acts 20:21
[39] Hebrews 4:16
[40] Luke 11:9, 13
[41] Luke 11:10 (emphasis added)
[42] Mark 11:24 (emphasis added)
[43] Acts 2:4

3. Move into action. Once you have fully committed yourself to God and His work, and have been empowered by God's Spirit, immediately begin to tell others about Christ. Make it your aim to learn how to walk daily in the Spirit's presence and power.[44] Commit yourself to devoted prayer and diligent Bible study. And begin giving generously to God's work. If you sense that God is calling you into ministry, don't be afraid. Say "Yes!" to His call. He who has called you will make a way for you to move forward.

Review and Application

Paul informed the believers in Corinth, "The time is short."[45] He wanted them to know that Jesus could come at any moment. Because of this, they were not to live self-indulgent lives. Rather, they were to fully commit themselves to the Lord's work. Pentecostal women must do the same. They must get busy doing the work Jesus has called them to do. With this in mind, take a few moments to reflect, apply, and implement the things you have learned.

Reflect:

Reflect on the following issues:

- Name some notable Old Testament and New Testament women God used to advance His kingdom.
- According to Acts 1:8, what qualifies women to participate in Spirit-empowered ministry?
- How does our Pentecostal heritage commend women as effective ministers of the gospel?

---

[44] Galatians 5:25. Note: Denzil R. Miller's helpful e-book, *In Step with the Spirit: Studies in the Spirit-Filled Walk,* is available for free download at www.DecadeofPentecost.org/e-books/

[45] 1 Corinthians 7:29 (NIV)

Apply:

Now, make the following applications to your present ministry:

- Evaluate your church or ministry. How open is your church to allowing Spirit-filled women to fully participate in gospel ministry?
- What adjustments need to be made in order to open the door for women to enter ministry?
- Women, what should you be doing to qualify yourselves as full participants in God's mission?

Commit:

Finally, pray this prayer and make this commitment:

- *Prayer:* "Lord, as a woman of God, I commit myself to you and your mission for the nations. To fulfill this commitment, I will need your Spirit. I therefore ask you to fill me with your Spirit and empower me to do your will."
- *Commitment:* "I commit myself to God and to His mission to redeem all people. With God's help, and in the Spirit's power, I will do my best to fulfill this sacred vow."

~ Chapter 11 ~

THE PENTECOSTAL BIBLE SCHOOL[1]

More than anything else, our Assemblies of God Bible schools across Africa hold the key to the future of the movement. Any national church wanting to mobilize themselves for effective Spirit-empowered witness, church planting, and missions must give serious attention to their ministerial training systems, for out of these institutions will come laborers for the harvest. We must therefore ensure that our Bibles schools are distinctly Pentecostal and truly missional, and that graduates from these institutions are thoroughly equipped to advance God's mission at home and to the ends of the earth in Pentecostal power.[2]

In this lesson, we will look into four key components of a truly Pentecostal Bible school: its *mission,* its *ethos,* its *curriculum,* and its *spiritual life.*

---

[1] I acknowledge John L. Easter's important contribution to this lesson. Dr. Easter is director of Africa's Hope.

[2] 2 Timothy 3:17

The Mission of the Pentecostal Bible School

Any school intent on producing effective Pentecostal leaders must understand and clearly define its mission. And it is important that this mission be expressed in a written mission statement. A mission statement is a public declaration of a school's *raison d'être,* or reason for being. A good mission statement succinctly declares why the school exists and what it intends to accomplish. For example, the mission statement of the Acts in Africa Initiative (the ministry that produced this book) is "Mobilizing the church for Spirit-empowered mission." Our AIA team members often remind themselves of this statement. This helps keep us focused on what God has called us to do.

The mission of the Pentecostal Bible school is to serve its national church by helping it fulfill its God-ordained mission. The goals of the Pentecostal Bible school ought to include the following:

1. Keepers of the flame. As "keeper of the flame," a chief goal of the Pentecostal Bible school is to ensure that the national church it serves remains authentically Pentecostal. In Chapter 3, we outlined what this means. We said that an authentic Pentecostal church is a Spirit-empowered missionary church. It is a church that takes its cue from the church described in the book of Acts. It therefore proclaims the *same message,* shares the *same mission,* embraces the *same experiences,* and employs the *same methods,* as did the church in Acts.

A truly Pentecostal Bible school will do the same. It will produce pastors and leaders who will lead their churches into genuine New Testament teaching, experience, and practice. Pentecostal Bible schools are to be crucibles in which truly Spirit-empowered Pentecostal ministers are forged. Someone has rightly said, "As goes the Bible school, so goes the church." If our churches are to remain truly Pentecostal and fearlessly missional, our Bible schools must set themselves as "keepers of the flame" of authentic New Testament Pentecostalism.

2. Sustainers of the mission. Second, our Pentecostal Bible schools are to serve the church as "sustainers of the mission." Pentecostal educators must never lose sight of the church's mission, and they must constantly remind the church why it exists. We discussed God's mission, or the *missio Dei,* in Chapter 1. We said that God's mission is to redeem and call unto himself a people out of every tribe, language, and nation on earth.[3] God raised up the church to join Him in this mission. The Pentecostal Bible school exists to train leaders who will ensure that the church remains true to that mission.

In the Great Commission, Jesus commanded His church to go "and make disciples of all nations." He further charged them to teach those disciples "to observe all that I have commanded you."[4] Then, before returning to His Father, Jesus ordered His disciples to remain in Jerusalem until they were "clothed with power from on high."[5] Pentecostal Bible school administrators and teachers must see themselves as "sustainers of the mission." As such, they exist to ensure that their students understand God's mission, are empowered by God's Spirit, and share God's passion to redeem the nations.

3. Developers of the mission force. Finally, Pentecostal Bible schools are to be "developers of the mission force." Administrators and teachers must ensure that those they train and deploy into the field are "competent ministers…of the Spirit."[6] In other words, they must ensure that their graduates have been filled with the Spirit and know how to maintain a daily walk with the Spirit.[7] They must further ensure that graduates are able to effectively minister in the power of the Holy Spirit. They must know how to heal the sick, cast out

---

[3] Cf., Revelation 5:9; 7:9
[4] Matthew 28:19-20
[5] Luke 24:49; cf. Acts 1:4-5,8
[6] 2 Corinthians 3:6
[7] Acts 1:4-5; Galatians 5:25

demons, and lead Christians into the fullness of the Holy Spirit.[8] Further, graduates from our Bible schools must be committed to extending God's kingdom by planting Spirit-empowered missionary churches at home, across Africa, and to the ends of the earth. Finally, they must be equipped to lead their churches to fully participate in the missions program of their national churches.

The Ethos of the Pentecostal Bible School

Not only must our Bible schools be Pentecostal in mission, they must be Pentecostal in ethos. *Ethos* refers to the atmosphere or culture of a school. It includes the underlying values, attitudes, and practices that define life in the community. In Acts 1:8 Jesus established two core cultural norms for the church. He determined that the church would function as a culture of the Spirit ("But you will receive power when the Holy Spirit has come upon you…") and a culture of mission ("…and you will be my witnesses…to the end of the earth"). These same cultural norms should define our Pentecostal Bible schools today.

1. Culture of the Spirit. Just as the presence of the Lord filled the temple in Jerusalem, the Spirit of the Lord must fill our Bible schools.[9] No Bible school can truly call itself Pentecostal if it lacks the manifest presence of the Lord. Administration, faculty, and student leaders must work together to cultivate such a culture of the Spirit. They must commit themselves to do whatever is necessary to ensure the Spirit's presence in every facet of campus life. (We will discuss this more in the last section of this chapter, "The Spiritual Life of the Pentecostal Bible School.")

2. Culture of mission. The Pentecostal Bible school must also embody a culture of mission. As discussed above, the school exists to help the church fulfill God's mission in the earth. Creating a culture

---

[8] Matthew 10:8
[9] 2 Chronicles 5:13-14

of mission requires that everyone in the school, including the administration, teachers, and students, all understand the church's mission, and that they are fully committed to the same. As mentioned above, to make this happen, the school must develop a mission statement in harmony with the mission of the church. This statement should be prominently displayed and often repeated in the school. Every faculty member and student must be able to recite the statement. Above all, they must wholeheartedly embrace its mission.

I remember how our mission statement helped to focus and energize the Assemblies of God School of Theology in Lilongwe, Malawi, where I taught for ten years.[10] The school's statement read, "Biblical training to touch the nations in the power of the Holy Spirit." The students often repeated this statement in class and chapel services, sometimes in several languages. Everyone in the school understood that they were there to learn God's Word and to prepare themselves to advance God's mission in Malawi and to the ends of the earth in Pentecostal power. As students graduated and went out from the school, the same passion was transferred to the churches. As a result, revival came to the Malawi Assemblies of God. This revival helped to spawn a mighty church planting movement with hundreds of new churches being planted in Malawi and neighboring countries.

Unless our schools fully embrace God's Spirit and mission, our training becomes purely academic, and our schools exist only to issue diplomas and produce "professional clergymen" who are largely ineffective in building God's kingdom. We must therefore create and maintain a culture of the Spirit and a culture of mission in our Pentecostal Bible schools.

---

[10] The school is now called the Malawi Assemblies of God Institute of Theology (MAGIT).

The Curriculum of the Pentecostal Bible School

Further, if our churches are to mobilize themselves for effective end-time mission, we must ensure that the curriculum we offer in our Bible schools is thoroughly Pentecostal.[11] Broadly speaking, a school's curriculum includes everything the school does to enhance the students' development. More particularly, curriculum refers to the subject matter taught in the various courses offered by the school. By "Pentecostal curriculum," we mean those courses, practices, and activities which uniquely emphasize the missional work of the Holy Spirit in and through the lives of Christians.

In developing our schools' curricula, we would be foolish to assume that two or three courses on Pentecostal themes will be enough to produce truly Pentecostal ministers—that is, ministers who are focused on reaching the nations with the gospel and able to minister in the power and anointing of the Spirit. An occasional course on "Pneumatology" or "Pentecostal Doctrine" will never suffice. We must offer ample courses dealing with essential Pentecostal related themes. Subject matter must include the following:

- A comprehensive study of missional pneumatology[12]
- A course covering a Pentecostal interpretation of the kingdom of God[13]

---

[11] For an extended discussion on this topic, see the author's book, *Teaching in the Spirit,* 28-41. Available on the internet at www.DecadeofPentecost.org.

[12] Mark R. Turney's book, *Encountering God's Missionary Spirit: A Missional Study of the Holy Spirit,* is available on the internet at www.DecadeofPentecost.org.

[13] The author's book, *The Kingdom and the Power: A Missional Study of the Holy Spirit* is available on the internet at DecadeofPentecost.org.

- A practical course on Spirit-empowered ministry[14]
- A study on how to live the Spirit-empowered life[15]
- A study on the book of Acts from a Pentecostal and missional perspective[16]
- A comprehensive study of Spirit baptism
- A study on divine healing and faith dynamics.

Further, we must purposefully "Pentecostalize" and "missionize" every course taught in our ministerial training institutions. In other words, we must reexamine every course, no matter what the subject, to ensure that each one contains the necessary pneumatological and missiological emphasis.

In all we do, we must never forget the most important factor in Pentecostal training is the Pentecostal teacher. As mentioned above, curriculum is more than just what is taught from books. The greatest influence on the students comes from the lives of the teachers. National church leaders and school administrators must therefore ensure that teachers are Spirit-filled and understand how to teach and minister in the Spirit's power.

The Spiritual Life of the Pentecostal Bible School

Finally, if we are to successfully mobilize our churches for Spirit-empowered mission, we must give attention to the spiritual life of our Bible schools and of the students attending these schools. Our schools must be places where the Spirit of God is manifestly present.

---

[14] The author's book, *Power Encounter: Ministering in the Power and Anointing of the Holy Spirit,* is available on the internet at DecadeofPentecost.org.

[15] The author's book, *In Step with the Spirit: Studies in the Spirit-filled Walk,* is available on the internet at www.DecadeofPentecost.org.

[16] The author's book, *The Spirit of God in Mission: A Vocational Study of the book of Acts: A Vocational Commentary on the book of Acts,* is available on the internet at www.DecadeofPentecost.org.

While we aim for academic excellence, this must not be our primary concern. Our primary concern is the moral and spiritual development of the students. If we are to train truly Pentecostal ministers, we must take seriously the importance of their spiritual formation. True spiritual formation can only occur in an atmosphere infused with the Spirit of God. Therefore, the spiritual atmosphere of the school is a primary concern.

One indicator of the spiritual life of our schools is our daily chapel services. We must work to ensure that our chapel services are permeated with the Spirit's presence and focused on fulfilling God's mission. If they are not, we must move quickly to remedy this shortcoming. This daily service in our Bible schools must be more than just a devotional time, or even worse, a time for school announcements. It must become a dynamic spiritual laboratory where students encounter the living God and learn how to respond to and move in the power of the Holy Spirit. It should be a place where teachers model Spirit-empowered ministry through their anointed preaching and the manifestation of spiritual gifts. The school must further conduct at least one spiritual emphasis week each term. These events should emphasize the work of the Spirit in missions. Students must be given frequent opportunities to respond to the call of God and be filled and refilled with the Holy Spirit.

Finally, the atmosphere of the school must be pervaded by prayer. Class sessions should begin and end with prayer. If necessary, chapel times must be extended to allow time for prayer at the altars. Prayer groups should be organized and supported. For example, there could be an "Unreached Tribes Prayer Group," or a "Church Planting Prayer Group," or a "Pentecostal Revival Prayer Group." Teachers and administrators must lead the way in modeling lives of committed prayer.

Chapter 11: The Pentecostal Bible School

Review and Application

We have learned that an authentically Pentecostal Bible school is essential to mobilizing a national church for Spirit-empowered missions and church planting. We have further learned what such a Bible school looks like. It is empowered by God's Spirit and focused on His mission. This twofold focus pervades the schools culture, its curriculum, and its spiritual life.

Let's now take a moment to reflect on what we have learned in this lesson and to commit ourselves to deliberately training authentic Pentecostal ministers.

Reflect:

Reflect on the following issues. Based on what you have learned in this lesson…

- Describe the threefold *mission* of a truly Pentecostal Bible school.
- Describe the twofold *ethos* of a truly Pentecostal Bible school.
- Describe the *curriculum* of a truly Pentecostal Bible school.
- Describe the *spiritual life* of a truly Pentecostal Bible school.

Apply:

Now, make the following applications. Based on what you have learned in this lesson…

- Evaluate your schools mission statement.
- Evaluate your school's Pentecostal and missional ethos.
- Evaluate your school's curriculum.
- Evaluate your school's spiritual life.

Commit:

Finally, pray this prayer and make this commitment:

- *Prayer:* "Lord, send your Spirit to empower and guide our Bible schools. Give us the will and the wisdom we need to revive and reshape our schools into authentic Pentecostal training institutions."
- *Commitment:* "We commit our Bible schools to God and to His mission. We will do whatever is necessary to ensure that they are authentically Pentecostal in mission, ethos, curriculum, and spiritual life."

– Chapter 12 –

THE PENTECOSTAL LEADER[1]

Mobilizing the church for Spirit-empowered mission will require effective leadership—the kind of leadership exhibited by Jesus and the apostles in the New Testament. Initially, Jesus led the mission. He began by calling disciples and charging them, "Follow me, and I will make you fishers of men."[2] Later, after His death and resurrection, He handed over this leadership role to His apostles. He told them, "As the Father has sent me, even so I am sending you."[3] Later, Paul, who was himself chosen by Christ, taught that the church was to be led by apostles, prophets, evangelists, pastors, and teachers whom Christ himself gives to the church. Their

---

[1] Many of concepts in this lesson were presented in lectures by AIA team member, Dr. Enson Lwesya, in Acts 1:8 Conferences across Africa.

[2] Matthew 4:19

[3] John 20:21

job is "to equip the saints for the work of ministry, for building up the body of Christ."[4]

Jesus modeled the kind of leadership needed to direct His church. Through word and example, He showed that those who lead the church must themselves be led by the Spirit. He chose to fulfill His ministry in the power of, and under the direction of, the Holy Spirit. As He began His ministry, Jesus announced,

> "The Spirit of the Lord is upon me, because he has anointed me to proclaim good news to the poor. He has sent me to proclaim liberty to the captives and recovering of sight to the blind, to set at liberty those who are oppressed, to proclaim the year of the Lord's favor."[5]

Peter once referred to Jesus as our "Leader and Savior."[6] He later described Jesus' leadership style like this: "God anointed Jesus of Nazareth with the Holy Spirit and with power. He went about doing good and healing all who were oppressed by the devil, for God was with him."[7] The true Pentecostal leader will seek to model his or her leadership style on that of Jesus. Jesus said, "A disciple is not above his teacher, but everyone when he is fully trained will be like his teacher."[8]

The apostle Paul is another good example of an authentic Pentecostal leader. In Acts, Luke presents Paul as a charismatically gifted, Spirit-led leader. He tells how, on one occasion, the Holy Spirit directed Paul and his missionary team into Europe through a night vision. Luke writes, "After Paul had seen the vision, we got

---

[4] Ephesians 4:11-12
[5] Luke 4:17-18
[6] Acts 5:31
[7] Acts 10:38
[8] Luke 6:40

ready at once to leave for Macedonia, concluding that God had called us to preach the gospel to them."[9]

During this same journey, Paul led his missionary team to Corinth where he planted a church.[10] In his follow-up letter to the church, Paul reminded them how he conducted himself while there: "I came to you in weakness and fear, and with much trembling. My message and my preaching were not with wise and persuasive words, but with a demonstration of the Spirit's power."[11] He then urged the Corinthian Christians, "Be imitators of me, as I am of Christ."[12]

In this lesson, we will discuss Pentecostal leadership. We will present a model based on the leadership methods of Jesus and the apostles. In doing this, we will first define what it means to lead "Pentecostally." We will then discuss some of the qualities and activities of authentic Pentecostal leaders.

Defining Pentecostal Leadership

Someone once said about Pentecostal leadership, "It's the same thing, only different!" By this, he meant that Pentecostal leaders employ many of the same leadership methods as do non-Pentecostal leaders; and yet, there are some important differences. A Pentecostal leader's approach is significantly shaped by his or her experience with the Spirit. The Pentecostal leader's unique understanding of how the Spirit works in his or her life, and in the lives of others, profoundly affects the way they lead.

A Pentecostal leader is a God-chosen man or woman who has been filled with the Spirit and consciously seeks the wisdom and guidance of the Spirit. His or her goal is to influence a specific group

---

[9] Acts 16:10
[10] Paul's team included Silas, Timothy, and Luke.
[11] 1 Corinthians 2:3-4
[12] 1 Corinthians 11:1

of God's people to faithfully and effectively fulfill their God-ordained role in advancing His mission in the earth. Let's break down our definition into its component parts.

1. Called by God. First, truly Pentecostal leaders have been called by God and chosen by Him to lead His people. They have neither called nor appointed themselves. Because of this, they profoundly relate to Paul, who identified himself as "a servant of Christ Jesus, called to be an apostle, set apart for the gospel of God."[13]

2. Full of the Spirit. Next, the Pentecostal leader has been filled with the Spirit and seeks to live his or her life under the Spirit's influence.[14] They take seriously Christ's command to "stay in the city until you are clothed with power from on high,"[15] and Paul's command, "Be [continually] filled with the Spirit."[16]

3. Seeks God's guidance. Third, Pentecostal leaders proactively seek the Spirit's guidance in all they do. They understand that their chief duty is to carry out God's will as revealed in Scripture and by the Holy Spirit. The authentic Pentecostal leader will therefore spend much time in Bible study and prayer.

4. Influence God's people. Finally, the Pentecostal leader seeks to influence a specific group of God's people, such as a national or local church, to faithfully and effectively fulfill their God-ordained role in advancing God's mission in the earth.

Qualities of the Pentecostal Leader

---

[13] Romans 1:1
[14] Galatians 5:25
[15] Luke 24:49
[16] Ephesians 5:18 (literal translation); cf. Acts 13:52 (NASB)

At a bare minimum, the authentic Pentecostal leader must be born of the Spirit,[17] filled with the Spirit,[18] and able to lead others into the Spirit-empowered walk.[19] They must be able to discern the voice of the Spirit and be proficient in the ministry of spiritual gifts.[20] They must understand, and be committed to, the mission of God.[21] And they must be ready to lay down their life for the cause of Christ, should such a sacrifice be required.[22]

Five distinctive qualities mark the authentic Pentecostal leader, including integrity, understanding, commitment, focus, and capacity. Let's look at each of these qualities:

1. Integrity. Above all else, authentic Pentecostal leaders must strive to live godly, Christ-honoring lives. In God's work, nothing is more important. Sadly, far too many Pentecostal churches and organizations are plagued with corrupt men and women who, because of their strong personalities, have achieved celebrity in the movement. These "wolves in sheep's clothing" bring shame on the church.[23] The Bible speaks of such godless people.

Paul warned the Ephesian elders of "fierce wolves" who would come in and ravage the flock of God.[24] In the same message, he reminded them of how he had led them with integrity. "I coveted no one's silver or gold or apparel," he said.[25] In similar manner, He reminded the Thessalonians of his godly conduct among them, saying, "You are witnesses, and God also, how holy and righteous

---

[17] John 3:3, 7
[18] Acts 1:4-5, 8; 2:4
[19] Acts 1:8; 8:17-18; 19:1-7
[20] John 5:19; Romans 8:14; Acts 16:6-10
[21] Hebrews 10:7; Mark 10:28
[22] John 10:11-13; Revelation 12:11
[23] Matthew 7:15
[24] Acts 20:29
[25] Acts 20:33

and blameless was our conduct toward you believers."[26] Paul is a good example of an authentic Pentecostal leader. He not only led with authority, and ministered with power, he lived with godly integrity.

2. Understanding. Second, an authentic Pentecostal leader must clearly understand his or her God-given responsibilities. They must faithfully serve Christ and His church, leading God's people to advance His mission in the power of the Holy Spirit. Pentecostal leaders gain this understanding from two sources: God's Word and God's Spirit. By faithfully studying Scripture, they come to understand God's mission to redeem the nations. By praying and being attentive to God's voice, they come to understand their unique role in fulfilling that mission.

Jesus clearly understood His place in God's redemptive plan. He often spoke of His mission. He declared, "For the Son of Man came to seek and to save the lost."[27] He prayed to His Heavenly Father, "I have come to do your will, O God."[28] In similar fashion, Paul understood his unique role in God's work. He wrote, "For this I was appointed a preacher and an apostle…a teacher of the Gentiles in faith and truth."[29] Like Jesus and Paul, through daily prayer and Bible study, the authentic Pentecostal leader will seek to gain greater understanding of God's mission, and his or her role in fulfilling that mission.

3. Commitment. Not only must the authentic Pentecostal leader understand God's mission, he or she must be fully committed to the same. In previous lessons, we have defined the mission of God as God's purpose and work in the world in relation to fallen humanity. His mission is to redeem and call unto himself a people out of every kindred, tongue, and nation on earth. The authentic Pentecostal leader

---

[26] 1 Thessalonians 2:10
[27] Luke 19:10; cf. Mark 10:45; John 6:38; 18:37
[28] Hebrews 10:7
[29] 1 Timothy 2:7

is committed to—and remains unswervingly focused on—leading the church to fulfill that mission.

While others' thoughts may wander, the true Pentecostal leader's attention remains focused on fulfilling God's will for themselves and for the people they lead. All their thoughts and actions move in the direction of God's mission. They understand the bigger picture, God's redemptive plan for the nations. They also understand where their church or group fits into that grand picture. Then, they unswervingly lead the church in that direction.

4. Anointing. True Pentecostal leaders rely heavily on the Holy Spirit to anoint, enable, and guide them in ministry. They seek to follow the example of Jesus, who was himself anointed and led by the Holy Spirit.[30] They further take seriously the Master's parting words to His disciples, when He commanded them not to begin their ministries until they had been empowered by the Holy Spirit.[31] On that same occasion Jesus promised them, "But you will receive power when the Holy Spirit has come upon you, and you will be my witnesses..."[32] The authentic Pentecostal leader thus cherishes the Spirit's anointing, and he or she endeavors to maintain the touch of the Spirit on their lives through committed prayer, holy living, and humble service.[33]

5. Humility. True Pentecostal leaders rightly see themselves as servants of God, His people, and His mission. They seek to follow the example of the Lord, who humbled himself and became a servant, even to the point of dying on the cross.[34] Jesus further taught His disciples, "Whoever would be great among you must be your servant, and whoever would be first among you must be slave of all. For even

---

[30] Luke 3:21-22; 4:1, 18-19;
[31] Acts 1:4-5; cf. Luke 24:49
[32] Acts 1:8
[33] 1 Corinthians 12:31; 14:1
[34] Philippians 2:7-8

the Son of Man came not to be served but to serve, and to give his life as a ransom for many."[35] This kind of leadership is called *servant leadership*. Conversely, the leader who exalts himself or herself and seeks to exploit God's people can never be called a true Pentecostal leader. They are rather "wolves in sheep's clothing"[36] The Bible tells us to "Have nothing to do with such people."[37]

6. *Competency*. The authentic Pentecostal leader will strive for competency. He or she realizes that, while being a good person is essential, it is not enough. Africans are known for being good, humble, and hospitable. To be a good leader, however, requires that one develop certain skills. These skills include the ability to teach, to cast vision, to motivate others, and to organize the work.

The Pentecostal leader further realizes that, ultimately, leadership ability comes from God through the Holy Spirit. Paul was acutely aware of this. He explained to the Corinthians, "Not that we are competent in ourselves to claim anything for ourselves, but our competence comes from God. He has made us competent as ministers...of the Spirit."[38] Paul called this competency *grace*. He wrote, "Grace was given to each one of us according to the measure of Christ's gift."[39] The authentic Pentecostal leader will relentlessly look to God for such competency.

Activities of the Pentecostal Leader

The Pentecostal leader must not be like the pastor who was seen running behind his congregation shouting, "Wait for me, I'm your leader!" On the contrary, he or she is called to go in front and invite others to follow. As mentioned above, Peter once referred to Jesus as

---

[35] Mark 10:43-45
[36] Matthew 7:15-16; Acts 20:29-30
[37] 2 Timothy 3:5 (NIV)
[38] 2 Corinthians 3:5-6 (NIV)
[39] Ephesians 4:7

our "Leader and Savior."[40] As such, Jesus commanded His disciples, "Follow me, and I will make you become fishers of men."[41] In like manner, Paul admonished the Christians in Corinth, "Follow my example, as I follow the example of Christ."[42] True Pentecostal leaders thus initiate God-inspired programs and strategies and inspire others to follow.

The Pentecostal leader is also a follower. They gladly follow those whom the Holy Spirit has placed over them. They are also followers of the Spirit himself. They obey Paul's admonition to the Ephesian elders, "Pay careful attention to yourselves and to all the flock, in which the Holy Spirit has made you overseers."[43]

Effective Pentecostal leaders lead their churches in fulfilling the mission of God in at least three critical ways: by vision casting, by supervising the work, and by perpetuating the vision. Let's look more closely at these essential leadership activities.

1. Vision casting. Pentecostal leaders cast a vision of a preferred future for the church or organization they lead. In doing this, they help God's people to see the future God has ordained for them. They then influence the people to move in that God-ordained direction. They cast the vision with their words, their actions, and their attitudes. Their God-inspired dream so consumes them that they cannot let it go. As a result, they talk, and talk, and talk about the vision. Spirit-inspired passion flows from their lives.

Authentic Pentecostal leaders do not promote their own vision of the future. They rather promote God's vision as revealed in His Word and through His Spirit. The Bible tells us, "Where there is no vision, the people perish."[44] The word for *vision* in this verse speaks of

---

[40] Acts 5:31
[41] Mark 1:17
[42] 1 Corinthians 11:1 (NIV)
[43] Acts 20:28
[44] Proverbs 29:18 (KJV)

prophetic insight. The ESV translates this verse, "Where there is no prophetic vision the people cast off restraint," or as the margin reads, "the people are discouraged." Such discouragement often results in self-absorption, decline, and eventually destruction. A well-communicated vision will cause the people to understand five things:

- *Who they are.* They are God's Spirit-empowered missionary people, commissioned by Christ to do His bidding in the earth.
- *Where they must go.* They are to move together to fulfill God's mission by winning the lost, planting new churches, and participating in sending missionaries to the nations.
- *What they must do.* They must be empowered by God's Spirit and committed to doing their part in fulfilling God's mission.
- *How they are going to do it.* The leader must articulate a specific plan and program of how to accomplish the work. He or she must then show the people how they will engage in the work.
- *How they must begin.* The effective Pentecostal leader will assign individual tasks to help the people begin well.

Sadly, however, many God-given dreams die in the heart of the leader. The Pentecostal leader must not let this happen. He or she must stand tall and boldly tell the people, "This is the way, walk in it."

As Jesus was about to ascend into heaven, He restated His vision for His church. He told His disciples, "But you will receive power when the Holy Spirit has come upon you, and you will be my witnesses in Jerusalem and in all Judea and Samaria, and to the end of the earth."[45] Jesus was telling His team that the church existed to

---

[45] Acts 1:8

fulfill God's mission, and that mission can be fulfilled only through the Spirit's power.

2. Supervising. Pentecostal leaders not only cast vision, they supervise the fulfillment of the vision. Between discovering where God wants us to be and arriving at our destination, there is a pathway. Pentecostal leaders guide God's people along that way. This is what Jesus did. He cast the vision and then implemented a strategy to fulfill the vision. His strategy was to call men and women to His side, train them, commission them, empower them, and then to deploy them to the work. Pentecostal leaders must do the same. They do this through Spirit-guided planning, mobilization, and supervision.

Thus, the Pentecostal leader is not only a leader, he or she is a manager. As managers, they organize the church for Spirit-empowered mission. They oversee the tactics and activities necessary to execute the plan. These activities include recruiting, planning, training, and deploying workers to the field. In all of this, the Pentecostal leader depends on the Spirit for insight and direction,

3. Perpetuation. Pentecostal leaders also shoulder the important responsibility of perpetuating and expanding the missionary vision of the group. One way they do this is by raising up other visionary Pentecostal leaders. To fail in this area is to fail utterly. If other leaders are not recruited and developed, the vision will die, and the mission will cease. How sad that so many God-ordained ministries have died with their founders because these founders failed to adequately instill the vision in others.

Jesus was serious about perpetuating His vision in others. Soon after He began His ministry, He started calling disciples. The Bible says, "He appointed twelve (whom he also named apostles) so that they might be with him and he might send them out to preach..."[46] These men would carry on the work after He was gone. He then trained them, empowered them, and then sent them out to do the same

---

[46] Mark 3:14; cf. 1:16-17; 2:13-14; 3:13-19

with others. He commissioned them to "go…and make disciples of all nations…"[47] In other words, they were to carry the vision forward after He had departed. They were to do with others what He had done with them.

Paul followed Jesus' example. He did not carry out His missionary ministry alone, but invited others to join him. He then mentored and trained them, just as Jesus had done with His disciples. Paul's disciples included John Mark, Timothy, Titus, Luke and others. He instructed Timothy to do with others as he had done with him. "What you have heard from me," he told his son in the faith, "entrust to faithful men who will be able to teach others also."[48] If we want to perpetuate the vision, we must follow in the footsteps of Jesus and Paul.

What definite steps can we take to perpetuate the vision of Pentecostal mission today? We can be the kind of person others want to follow. Paul admonished the believers in Thessalonica, "You yourselves know how you ought to imitate us," because, he said, we gave you "an example to imitate."[49] Be a man or woman of God that others will want to emulate, a person of honor, integrity, and vision. Then, take notice of those in your church in whom God is working, and invest in them. Schedule time to pray with them and teach them how to be effective leaders themselves. When possible, invite them to join you in ministry.

Review and Application

Now that you have completed this lesson, take a few moments to reflect, apply, and implement the things you have learned.

Reflect:

---

[47] Matthew 28:19
[48] 2 Timothy 2:2
[49] 2 Thessalonians 3:7, 9

Chapter 12: The Pentecostal Leader

Reflect on the following issues:

- Identify and discuss some important differences between a Pentecostal leadership style and a non-Pentecostal leadership style.
- To whom does the Pentecostal leader look for a model of Spirit-enabled leadership? Explain your answer.
- List and discuss six qualities of a true Pentecostal leader.
- List and discuss three activities of Pentecostal leaders.

Apply:

Make the following applications to your present ministry:

- Based on what you have learned in this lesson, assess your own leadership style by answering the following questions:
    1. Am I daily walking in the Spirit, and do I consciously allow the Spirit to guide my leadership choices?
    2. How does by leadership style compare with the Spirit-enabled leadership styles of Jesus and the apostles?
    3. Can I truly say that my leadership style is characterized by integrity, understanding, commitment, anointing, humility, and competency?
- Now, begin to develop a strategy on how you can become a more authentic, more effective, Pentecostal leader.

Commit:

In closing, pray this prayer and make this commitment:

- *Prayer:* "Lord, I submit myself to you and your leadership. Fill me with the Spirit and make me an authentic Pentecostal leader."
- *Commitment:* "With God's help, I will be the authentic Pentecostal leader that is exemplified in the ministries of Jesus and the apostles."

Chapter 12: The Pentecostal Leader

~ Appendix 1 ~
# ACTS 1:8 CONFERENCE PLANNING GUIDE

Acts 1:8 Conferences have helped shape the face of the Africa Assemblies of God, making it into a more Pentecostal, more missional movement. In these conferences, Acts in Africa team members have seen thousands of believers baptized in the Holy Spirit and empowered as Christ's witnesses. We have watched in amazement as Assemblies of God churches across Africa have committed to plant thousands of new Spirit-empowered missionary churches and train thousands of Pentecostal pastors to care for those churches.

Pastors have asked, "Can I conduct an Acts 1:8 Conference in my local church?" The answer is, "Yes, you can!" A pastor can do it alone in his or her own local church. Or two or more pastors can join together to plan a joint conference for multiple churches. This Appendix is included in this book as a step-by-step guide to help you plan and conduct your own Acts 1:8 Conference.

1. **Benefits of a Local Acts 1:8 Conference**
   - The church will be strengthened.
     a. It will become more authentically Pentecostal and more committed to God's mission.
     b. It will become more effective in fulfilling its God-given mandate of reaching the lost in the power of the Holy Spirit.
   - Church members will be empowered.
     a. As church members are filled with the Spirit, they will be empowered as Christ's witnesses to the lost.
     b. They will be motivated to reach their friends, neighbors, and the nations with the gospel.
   - Church leaders will be challenged.

a. Leaders will be challenged to be filled with the Spirit and to live Spirit-empowered, Spirit-directed lives.
   b. They will be challenged to become more involved in the evangelism and church planting efforts of the church.
- The work of God will be advanced.
   a. God's people will be inspired to give more, pray more, and become more involved in God's work.
   b. As a result, the church will grow and become stronger.
   c. New churches will be planted.

2. **Understanding the Acts 1:8 Conference**
   - The Purpose of an Acts 1:8 Conference:
      a. The purpose of an Acts 1:8 Conference is to mobilize the church for Spirit-empowered evangelism, church planting, and missions.
      b. The entire conference is structured around Jesus' final message to the church found in Acts 1:8: "But you will receive power when the Holy Spirit has come upon you, and you will be my witnesses in Jerusalem and in all Judea and Samaria, and to the end of the earth."
      c. Every Acts 1:8 Conference will thus focus on the two emphases of Acts 1:8:
         1) The empowering of the Holy Spirit
         2) The witness of the church at home and to the ends of the earth.
   - Four Essential Elements of an Acts 1:8 Conference:
      a. Element 1: Intercessory prayer:
         1) Each day, the conference will begin with a time of intercessory prayer.
         2) Like the other elements of the conference, the prayer time will focus on the twofold emphasis of Acts 1:8: prayer for the Spirit—and prayer for the nations.
            ▶ *See Appendix 2: "Acts 1:8 Conference Prayer Guide"*

b. Element 2: Missional instruction:
   1) In the teaching sessions, the conference teachers will present the twelve lessons found in this book.
   2) Note how each lesson is based on Acts 1:8.
c. Element 3: Strategy development:
   1) In four strategy sessions, delegates will develop a missions mobilization strategy for their particular church or ministry.
   2) The strategy will be developed in discussion groups who will report back to the entire assembly.
   3) The four strategy sessions are as follows:
      a) Assessment: "Where are we now?"
      b) Goals: "Where does God want us to be?"
      c) Strategies: "How do we get there?"
      d) Commitment: "What commitments must we make?"
   ▶ *See Appendix 3: "Strategy Sessions Guide"*
d. Element 4: Holy Spirit empowerment:
   1) The conference will include evening (or afternoon) Holy Spirit Empowerment Services.
   2) In these services, presenters will preach sermons based on Acts 1:8 and then call the people forward to receive the Holy Spirit.
   ▶ *See Appendix 4: "Sermon Outlines for Acts 1:8 Conferences"*

3. **Planning an Acts 1:8 Conference** (Eight steps:)
   - Step 1: Decide to have an Acts 1:8 Conference.
   - Step 2: Set a date for the conference.
   - Step 3: Create a plan for the conference:
   a. What lessons will we teach?
   b. Who will be involved?
   c. Where will the conference be held?

d. Other pertinent issues.
▶ *See Appendix 5: "Typical Acts 1:8 Conference Schedules"*
- Step 4: Prepare your team:
  a. Assign and review team member responsibilities.
  b. Meet together for prayer and information sharing.
  ▶ *Resources are available at www.DecadeofPentecost.org.*
- Step 5: Pray for the conference:
  a. Prayer in regular church services.
  b. Develop local "Decade of Pentecost" prayer groups.
- Step 6: Promote the conference:
  a. Through church announcements
  b. Through other media: print, e-mail, radio, television, text messaging, social media, etc.
- Step 7: Conduct the conference (See item 4 below)
- Step 8: Follow-up:
  a. Implement the evangelism, church planting, training and missions strategies developed in the conference.
  b. See Item 5 below.

4. **Conducting the Acts 1:8 Conference**

   - During the conference, stay resolutely focused on what you are trying to accomplish, that is, mobilizing the church for Spirit-empowered mission.
   - Do not get sidetracked and wander off on tangents, but stay focused on the Acts 1:8 theme—empowerment for mission.
   - Trust God to pour out His Spirit on the church.

5. **After the Conference**

   - Take immediate action!
   - Continue to learn, teach, and preach the message of Acts 1:8.
   - Implement what you have learned by mobilizing the people for prayer, witness, church planting, and missions.

~ Appendix 2 ~
ACTS 1:8 CONFERENCE PRAYER GUIDE

If we are to experience a genuine move of the Spirit, we will need to pray. Prayer is therefore an essential element of every Acts 1:8 Conference. Prayer during the conference will include prayers of commitment following each teaching session and prayer to receive the Spirit during our Holy Spirit Empowerment Services. It will also include times of intercessory prayer in our Morning Prayer Sessions. As with every element of the conference, these prayer sessions will be modeled on Jesus' promise in Acts 1:8:

> "But you will *receive power* when the Holy Spirit has come upon you, and you will *be my witnesses* in Jerusalem and in all Judea and Samaria, and to the end of the earth."

In other words, in each session, we will pray for the Spirit to be outpoured, and we will pray for the lost to be evangelized.

On the following pages, you will find prayer guides to help give direction to the morning prayer sessions. Using these guides, the moderator will begin each session by introducing and explaining the purpose of that particular session. He or she will then lead the people step-by-step through each prayer point. You will notice that, in accordance with our Acts 1:8 theme, each day's prayer time is divided into two parts: "Prayer for the Spirit" and "Prayer for the Nations." Each part should take up about half of the prayer session.

While it is good to begin each morning's prayer session with a song or chorus, singing should be kept to a minimum with the bulk of the time being reserved for intercessory prayer. As with every session of the conference, the prayer meeting should begin and end on time.

Appendix 2: Acts 1:8 Conference Prayer Guide

Day 1 – Part 1:
Prayer for the Spirit: "Oh Lord, Empower Us Today"

Purpose: The purpose of this part of this prayer session is to intercede to God for this Acts 1:8 Conference. Our prayer is that the Holy Spirit will come upon us in power during our times together.

Prayer Points:

- Lord, send your Holy Spirit to anoint our Prayer Sessions.
- Lord, send your Holy Spirit to enlighten our Teaching Sessions.
- Lord, send your Holy Spirit to guide our Strategy Sessions.
- Lord, Send your Holy Spirit to empower us during our Holy Spirit Empowerment Services.
- Lord, Send your Holy Spirit on the churches of our city and country this coming Sunday.

Day 1 – Part 2:
Prayer for the Nations: "O Lord, Save the Unreached Peoples of the World"

Purpose: In our times of prayer for the nations. We will cry out to God to save the lost, and we will offer ourselves to God to reach them. According to the Joshua Project, there are more than 3 billion unreached people in the world, or 41% of the world's population. They comprise more than 7,000 people groups. In this session, we will intercede for the unreached peoples of the world.

Prayer Points:

- O Lord, save the world's least-reached peoples.
- O Lord, create in our hearts an awareness of those who are least-reached with the gospel.
- O Lord, create in our hearts a deep burden for these lost ones for whom you died.
- O Lord, give us the wisdom and courage we need to reach out to these unreached people.
- O Lord, fill us with your Spirit, and send laborers from our midst to the unreached peoples of the world.

Day 2 – Part 1:
Prayer for the Spirit: "O Lord, Empower Our Churches"

Purpose: There is a great need for our church(es) to be truly Pentecostal. And yet, only a small percentage of our people are Spirit-baptized. We must have a fresh Pentecostal outpouring in our churches with many of our members being baptized in the Holy Spirit. The purpose of this session it to intercede for such an outpouring on our churches.

Prayer Points:

- Lord, pour out your Spirit on the churches of Africa.
- Lord, pour out your Spirit on the churches in our country.
- Lord, pour out your Spirit on my local church.
- Lord, pour out your Spirit on me, so that I may help lead the church into Pentecostal revival.

Day 2 – Part 2:
Prayer for the Nations: "O Lord, Save the Unreached Tribes of Africa"

Purpose: According to the Joshua Project, there are more than 350 million unreached people in Africa, comprising more than 980 people groups, and making up about 30% of the population. In this session, we will intercede for Africa's unreached peoples.

Prayer Points:

- O Lord, save the unreached tribes of Africa.
- O Lord, open our eyes to the lost tribes of Africa in our own country and region.
- O Lord, help us to realize our responsibility to reach out to these neglected tribes with the gospel of Jesus Christ.
- O Lord, create in our hearts a burden to reach these lost peoples.
- O Lord, give us the wisdom to know what we must do to reach them.
- O Lord, fill us again with your Spirit, and move us into action to reach these lost tribes.

Day 3 – Part 1:
Prayer for the Spirit: "O Lord, Empower Our Pastors and Leaders"

Purpose: Our pastors and lay leaders are the key to seeing our people filled with the Spirit and the church mobilized for effective evangelism and missions. The purpose of this session is to intercede for these men and women. We will pray that they will be filled and refilled with the Spirit, and that they will become powerful proclaimers of Pentecost.

Prayer Points:

- Fill our pastor(s) again with your Holy Spirit.
- Empower them to preach your gospel to the lost.
- Empower them to lead their churches in to Pentecostal experience and practice.
- Empower them to lead their churches into powerful church planting and missions involvement.

Day 3 – Part 2:
Prayer for the Nations: "O Lord, Save the World of Islam"

Purpose: The world of Islam is perhaps the church's greatest missionary challenge. Today there are more than 1.5 billion Muslims in the world who desperately need the gospel of Jesus Christ. In this session, we will intercede for them.

Prayer Points:

- O Lord, save the world of Islam.
- O Lord, give us wisdom and understanding as to how we may best reach them.
- O Lord, help us to realize our responsibility before God to reach out to Muslims with the gospel.
- O Lord, give us wisdom and understanding as to how we may best reach them.
- O Lord, send out labors from our midst to the world of Islam.
- O Lord, put a burden in our heart for these Muslims in our midst.
- O Lord, fill us with your Spirit and move us into action to reach Muslims with the gospel.

Day 4 – Part 1:
Prayer for the Spirit: "O Lord, Empower Our Children and Young People"

Purpose: Should Jesus tarry His coming, our children and youth will soon lead our churches. They will be our pastors and church leaders. If they are not filled with the Spirit now, the future of our church is in peril. However, if they are powerfully filled with the Spirit, and properly discipled, our future is bright. The purpose of this session is to intercede for our children and the youth of our churches.

Prayer Points:
- Lord, send Pentecostal revival to the children and youth of Africa.
- Lord, pour out your Spirit and empower the children and youth of our churches. (Mention by name as many children and youth as you can remember.)
- Lord, empower and direct the children's and youth leaders of our churches. (Mention by name those youth leaders whom you know.)

Day 4 – Part 2:
Prayer for the Nations: "O Lord Send Us!"

Purpose: In previous sessions, we have interceded for the unreached peoples of the world, including the unreached tribes of Africa and the world of Islam. In this session, we will offer ourselves to God as His ambassadors to these peoples. And we will ask Him to empower us for the task.

Prayer Points:
- O Lord, send us to preach the gospel to the nations.
- O Lord, burden our churches and church leaders for missions.
- O Lord, give us the wisdom and grace we need to lead our churches into missions involvement.
- O Lord, empower me by your Spirit and send me!

Notes:

~ Appendix 3 ~
STRATEGY SESSIONS GUIDE

In the Strategy Sessions, conference delegates take what they have learned and experienced in the Teaching Sessions, Prayer Sessions, and Holy Spirit Empowerment Services, and apply these insights to their own ministry contexts. In these sessions, the conference leaders will lead them through a step-by-step process in which they develop real-world evangelism, church planting, and missions strategies. These Strategy Sessions occur each afternoon following the day's prayer and teaching sessions. They last from one to one and one half hours.

In the first session, delegates are divided into discussion groups of from 10-20 people each. Each group then quickly chooses their discussion leader and a recording secretary. The discussion leader will guide the group's conversation, and the recording secretary will record the decisions made by the group. They will later present their reports to the entire body.

The corporate goal of the strategy groups is to produce a united Acts 1:8 Declaration in which the church will commit themselves to specific spiritual, evangelistic, church planting, and missions goals. They will further develop a basic strategy for achieving the goals. This Acts 1:8 Declaration will be publically read, ratified, and signed during the Commitment Service at the close of the conference. It will then serve as a road map for the church's future ministry.

Development of the Acts 1:8 Declaration will proceed in a logical four-step sequence leading the church from where it is to where it needs to be. This sequence looks like this:

Assessment → Goals → Strategies → Commitment

Let's look more closely at this four-step process.

1. Assessment. In Strategy Session 1, the groups will assess the current state of the church based on Jesus' twofold mandate of Acts 1:8: "You will receive power" and "You will be my witnesses." In doing this, they will answer two pertinent questions: "How are we doing *Pentecostally?*" and "How are we doing *missionally?*" They will thus discuss how their church is doing in getting believers baptized in the Holy Spirit and how they are doing in fulfilling Christ's command to reach the lost. (See "Strategy Session 1: Assessment: "Where Are We Now?" below, for guidelines to this session.)

2. Goals. In Strategy Session 2, the discussion groups will prayerfully seek to answer the question, "Whet does God want us to be?" In doing this, they will develop specific evangelism, missions and church planting goals for their church. These goals will be presented to the entire delegation. Later, in the Implementation Session, leaders will review the goals presented by each group and develop the corporate goals to be included in the Acts 1:8 Declaration. (See "Strategy Session 2," below, for guidelines to this session.)

3. Strategies. In Strategy Session 3, the groups will meet to discuss the question, "What must we do?" In other words, what actions must we take if we are to achieve the goals we set in Session 2? The discussion will proceed as follows. Taking each projected goal, the group will discuss and recommend definite strategies that will need to be implemented fulfill each goal. As before, each recording secretary will present their groups conclusions to the entire delegation. (See Strategy Session 3: Strategy: "How Do We Get There?" below, for guidelines to this session.)

4. Commitment. In Strategy Session 4, the delegates will be dismissed and all reports handed over to the church leaders. The leaders will then set to review the reports and develop the Acts 1:8 Declaration which will be presented to the entire delegation for approval during the Commitment Service at the close of the conference. In that service, the Declaration will be read aloud and the delegates will be asked to approve the declaration by a voice vote. Select church leaders will then publically sign the Declaration. Finally, they will lay hands on the document and lead the congregation in prayer, pledging themselves to fulfilling the commitments made in the document. The Acts 1:8 Declaration will then serve as a plan for the church to move forward in mission. (See Strategy Session 4: Implementation: "Acts 1:8 Declaration Development," below, for guidelines to this session.)

Strategy Session 1:
Assessment: "Where Are We Now?"

Purpose of this session: The purpose of this session is to encourage the delegates to begin thinking about the present condition of their church (national or local) in terms of Jesus' mandate in Acts 1:8. They will evaluate the present depth of their church's emphasis (or non-emphasis) on missions and on Pentecostal experience.

Plan for this session: During this session, delegates will divide into discussion groups. They will evaluate their church in light of Jesus' two emphases in Acts 1:8:

- *The empowering of the Spirit:* "You will receive power when the Holy Spirit comes upon you..."[1]
- *The missionary mandate of the Church:* "...and you will be my witnesses in Jerusalem, and all Judea and Samaria, and to the ends of the earth."[2]

This assessment will aid the delegates in the discussions that will follow in Sessions 2-4.

---

[1] See also Luke 24:49 and Acts 1:4-5.
[2] See also Matt. 28:16-20; Mark 16:15-18.

Instructions to discussion groups: Evaluate and describe the current state of your church in relation to Jesus' final command to His disciples in Acts 1:8: In doing this you will be asking two questions and then rating your church on a scale from 1 to 10. You will then give three reasons why you gave your church that certain score.

Discussion Question 1: How is my church doing "Pentecostally"?

Based on Acts 1:8a ("You will receive power when the Holy Spirit comes upon you…"), discuss how your church is doing in getting members baptized in the Holy Spirit and empowered as Christ witnesses. Score from 1 to 10, with 1 indicating that we are doing very badly, and 10 indicating the we are doing great.

1 — 2 — 3 — 4 — 5 — 6 — 7 — 8 — 9 — 10
(The worse)   (The best)

Now, cite three reasons you gave your church or ministry the score you did:

1. Reason 1:
2. Reason 2:
3. Reason 3:

Discussion Question 2: How is my church doing missionally?
Based on Acts 1:8b ("You will be my witnesses in Jerusalem and in all Judea and Samaria, and to the end of the earth"), how are we doing in mobilizing ourselves, and our churches, for Spirit-empowered witness, church planting, and missions? Rate yourselves from 1 to 10, with 1 being the worse, and 10 being the best.

1 — 2 — 3 — 4 — 5 — 6 — 7 — 8 — 9 — 10
(The worse)   (The best)

Now, give three reasons you gave your church or ministry the score you did:

1. Reason 1:
2. Reason 2:
3. Reason 3:

Secretaries' reports: Following the group discussion, each recording secretary will go to the front of the church and read a brief summary of the group's conclusions to the entire congregation. Each report should take no more than 1-3 minutes.

Strategy Session 2:
Goals: "Where Does God Want Us to Be?"

Plan for this session: In the last strategy session, the discussion groups assessed the present state of the church. In this session, they will focus on the future. They will begin the process of setting missional goals for the church. In their groups, they will discuss where they believe the church should be in 1 to 10 years from now in the areas of Pentecostal experience and missions involvement. (Note: Church leaders will determine the number years the groups will use in setting their goals.)

Instructions to discussion groups: After dividing the delegates into their groups, have them discuss the following:

- How many people does God want to see baptized in the Holy Spirit and mobilized as witnesses, church planters, and cross-cultural missionaries?
- How many people does He want us to lead to Christ?
- How many new Spirit-empowered missionary churches does He want us to plant?
- How many does He want us to train in our Bible school(s)?
- How many people does He want us to mobilize as intercessory prayer warriors?
- Which unreached peoples (or places) does He want us to target?
- What other things does He want us to do?

Secretaries' reports: Each group secretary should now present a brief report of the group's conclusions to the entire delegation.

Strategy Session 3: Strategy: "How Do We Get There?"

Plan for this session: In this session, delegates will begin to develop a strategy (or plan) for achieving the goals they set in Session 2. Each discussion group will discuss what specific action steps the church needs to take to ensure they reach their goals laid out in the last session.

Instructions to discussion groups: As you develop your strategies for the missionary advance of the church, discuss the following:

- What definite actions will we take to fulfill each of our goals?
- Who will oversee/lead these efforts?
- What specific people or groups will we target?
- What forums will we use to fulfill our goals?
- At what times (or dates) will we schedule these efforts?
- What means will we use to achieve our goals?
- What media will we use to achieve our goals?

Secretaries' reports: Each group secretary should now present a brief report of the group's conclusions to the entire delegation. They will then hand over their reports to the church leadership.

Strategy Session 4: Commitment: "Acts 1:8 Declaration Development"

Plan for this session: The purpose of this session is to develop an "Acts 1:8 Declaration" that expresses the church's commitment to pursue these noble ends. Only the church leadership will participate in this discussion.

Instructions to leaders: In this session church leaders will review the reports from all the discussion groups developed in the first three sessions. Based on these reports and their own insights, they will develop an Acts 1:8 Declaration which will serve to motivate and guide the church in its evangelistic, missions, and church planting efforts.

Acts 1:8 Declaration: The declaration should contain the following elements:

1. A **preamble** naming the church and describing the occasion and date on which the Declaration was made. The preamble should express the church's commitment to fulfilling Christ's Great Commission in Pentecostal power.

2. A listing of **goals** the church commits itself to achieving by a certain date. These goals could include the following:

    - The number of believers the church intends to see baptized in the Holy Spirit and mobilized as Spirit-empowered witnesses
    - The number of new Spirit-empowered missionary churches the church intends to plant
    - The number of pastors, evangelists, and missionaries the church intends to deploy
    - The number of pastors and lay leaders the church intends to train
    - The number of souls the church intends to reach and add to the church
    - The number and names of the unreached people groups the church intends to engage
    - The number of intercessors the church intends to mobilize
    - Other missionary and outreach goals.

3. A brief description of the **strategies** the church intends to employ to achieve the above goals.

4. Spaces for the **signatures** of church leaders.

Ratifying the Declaration. The Declaration will be formally ratified in the Commitment Service at the close of the conference. There, the Declaration will be read to the delegates, and they will be asked to give their enthusiastic consent to it. The leaders will then publically sign the document and lead the congregation in a prayer of commitment.

~ Appendix 4 ~
SERMON OUTLINES FOR ACTS 1:8 CONFERENCES[1]

The Baptism in the Holy Spirit

Sermon in a Sentence: You can be baptized in the Holy Spirit today.
Purpose: To see believers baptized in the Holy Spirit and empowered as Christ's witness.
Text: Acts 1:8; 2:1-4
Introduction
1. There is nothing more important in the Christian's life than being baptized in the Spirit.
2. In this message we will answer three important questions concerning the baptism in the Holy Spirit.

I. WHAT IS THE BAPTISM IN THE HOLY SPIRIT?
A. It is a powerful, life-changing experience from God by which God clothes and fills a believer with His power and presence (Luke 24:49; Acts 1:8; Acts 2:1-4).
B. It is a promise for all believers (Acts 2:4; Acts 2:14-17; Acts 2:38-39).
C. It is a command to all believers (Acts 1:4-5; Ephesians 5:18).

II. WHY IS THE BAPTISM IN THE HOLY SPIRIT SO IMPORTANT IN EVERY BELIEVER'S LIFE?
A. Because it is the Christian's source of power for life and service (Acts 1:8; Acts 4:31-33).

---

[1] You can download for free three sermon outline books from the Decade of Pentecost website. Each book contains 100 outlines on the power of the Holy Spirit, Spirit-empowered missions, and intercessory prayer: www.DecadeofPentecost.org/sermon-outline-books/

B. Because, when you are baptized in the Holy Spirit, you will receive power to witness (Acts 1:8).
C. Because, when you are baptized in the Spirit, you will also receive power to do the following:
 1. Power to overcome temptation and live a holy life (Romans 1:4; 8:13).
 2. Power to pray more effectively (Luke 11:1-13; Romans 8:26-28).
 3. Power to love more ardently (Romans 5:5).
 4. Power to better understand the Word of God (1 Corinthians 2:14; John 14:26; 16:13).
 5. Power to preach more effectively (Acts 4:8, 31; 1 Corinthians 2:4).
 6. Power to do the works of Jesus (John 14:12 with John 14:16; 16:7).
 7. Power to more clearly discern the voice of God (Romans 8:16).
 8. Power to worship (John 4:24).

III. HOW CAN YOU BE FILLED WITH THE HOLY SPIRIT TODAY?
A. Three things you must do *before* you can be filled with the Spirit.
 1. You must be truly born again (Acts 2:38; John 14:17).
 2. You must hunger and thirst after God (Matthew 5:6; John 7:37).
 3. You must be prepared to witness for Christ (Acts 5:32).
B. You receive the Spirit through faith.
 1. Faith is the essential ingredient for receiving anything from God (Galatians 3:2, 5, 14).
 2. You must believe God for the Spirit (John 7:38).
C. Take these three steps of faith:
 1. *Ask* in faith (Luke 11:9, 13).
 2. *Receive* by faith (Luke 11:10; Mark 11:24).

3. *Speak* in faith: In faith, speak out of your innermost being (Acts 2:4; John 7:37).

Conclusion and Altar Call
Come now to be baptized in the Holy Spirit and empowered as Christ's witness.

Power with Purpose

Sermon in a Sentence: God wants to give you the Spirit to empower you to be His witness.

Sermon Purpose: That believers may understand the purpose of the baptism in the Holy Spirit and then be baptized in the Holy Spirit and empowered as Christ's witnesses.

Text: Acts 1:1-8

Introduction
1. In these last words of Jesus, He left His church with a purpose and power.
    a. *Its purpose:* "You will be my witnesses…to the ends of the earth" (Acts 1:8b; ref. Mark 15:15-16).
    b. *Its power:* "But you will receive power when the Holy Spirit comes upon you" (verse 8a; ref. Luke 24:48-49).
2. This text answers three questions about this "power with purpose":

I. WHO IS THE POWER FOR?
  A. The power is for "You." (Note: *"You* will receive power")
  B. This statement can apply to three "You's":
    1. *The specific you:* The first disciples (Acts 1:8).
    2. *The universal you:* All believers for the entire church age (Acts 2:38-39).
    3. *The personal you:* You who are here today! (Luke 11:13).

C. The power is not so much given *to* you as *through* you, to take the gospel to the nations!

II. WHEN IS THE POWER RECEIVED?
A. It is received "when the Holy Spirit comes upon you" (1:8).
B. The power was first received by the disciples when the Holy Spirit came upon them at Pentecost (Acts 2:1-4).
C. The power is received subsequent to salvation.
   1. The disciples were already saved when they received it.
   2. Spirit baptism is an experience separate from salvation.
   3. Its purpose is empowerment for mission.
D. Throughout Acts, the Spirit continued to come upon other believers with the same results—powerful witness.
   1. A second Jerusalem outpouring (Acts 4:31-33).
   2. Saul of Tarsus empowered (Acts 9:17-20).
   3. Believers in Ephesus empowered (Acts 19:6-7; 10).

III. WHY IS THE POWER GIVEN?
A. Note the phrase, "and you will be my witnesses" (Acts 1:8).
B. The power is given to empower disciples for witness!
   1. At Pentecost it resulted in powerful Spirit-anointed witness.
   2. 3000 were saved (Acts 2:39-41).
C. Spirit-empowered witness is the guiding theme of Acts.
   1. See: Acts 1:21; 2:32; 5:32; 10:38-41.
D. We have all been called to be Christ's witnesses, therefore, we must all receive the Spirit's power.

Conclusion and Altar Call

1. Come now and receive this "power with purpose" by being baptized in the Holy Spirit today.
2. How can you receive this power?
   a. *Ask* in faith (Luke 11:9, 10, 13).
   b. *Receive* by faith (Luke 11:10; Mark 11:24).
   c. *Speak* in faith (Acts 2:4).

Appendix 4: Sermon Outlines for Acts 1:8 Conferences

Fan Into Flame the Gift of God

Sermon in a Sentence: If we are to be effective witnesses, we must experience continual, personal Pentecostal revival.

Sermon Purpose: That people may understand how they can be continually filled and refilled with the Holy Spirit, and that they be filled or refilled today.

Text: 2 Timothy 1:6-8, 11-12, 14

Introduction
1. In our text, Paul tells Timothy how he can experience personal Pentecostal revival and why he needs to seek it.
2. He reminds Timothy to "fan into flames" the gift God had given him when Paul laid hands on him.
3. Paul is referring to the gift of the Spirit that Timothy received when he was baptized in the Holy Spirit.
4. This gift must be continually renewed.
5. Let's see how Paul defines revival in this passage.

I. ACCORDING TO THIS TEXT, TO EXPERIENCE PERSONAL PENTECOSTAL REVIVAL MEANS THREE THINGS:

A. It means to be personally filled with the Spirit (2 Timothy 1:6b).
  1. The "gift of God" spoken of in this text is the baptism in the Holy Spirit (Acts 1:4, 8:20, 11:17).
     a. Paul also includes himself as having received this gift. ("God gave *us* the Spirit...")
  2. Timothy was apparently filled with the Spirit when Paul laid hands on him and prayed for him.
     a. This likely happened in the church in Lystra that Paul started (Acts 14:8-20, 16:1-3).
  3. Spirit baptism following salvation was the pattern in the New Testament church (Acts 8:15-17; 9:17; 19:6).

- B. It means to consciously allow the Spirit to operate in one's life (2 Timothy 1:7).
    1. The Spirit's presence and work brings change in our lives.
    2. In the place of fear He brings power (Acts 1:8).
    3. He brings overflowing love (Romans 5:5).
    4. He brings self-control (Galatians 5:16).
- C. It means to be actively witnessing for Christ.
    1. Paul told Timothy, "Do not be ashamed to testify about our Lord" (2 Timothy 1:8).
    2. This reminds us of Christ's words in Acts 1:8.

II. THREE REASONS WE NEED TO EXPERIENCE PERSONAL REVIVAL:

- A. Because we will face opposition when we preach the gospel (2 Timothy 1:8, 11-12).
- B. Because we need the help of the Spirit to remain true to the gospel message and sound doctrine (2 Timothy 1:14).
- C. Because of our tendency to lose zeal for serving Christ (2 Timothy 1:6a).
    1. Paul tells Timothy to "stir up," or "rekindle," or "fan into flame," the gift of God which was in him.
    2. A fire must be stirred and fed or it will eventually go out.
    3. Many had abandoned Paul and turned back (2 Timothy 1:15; 4:10a).
    4. Paul was concerned that Timothy remain committed.
    5. We, too, must be vigilant to maintain our commitment to Christ and His mission by maintaining the presence of the Spirit in our lives.

III. TO EXPERIENCE PERSONAL PENTECOSTAL REVIVAL WE MUST DO SOMETHING

- A. Like Timothy, we must begin with a sincere faith in Christ (2 Timothy 1:5).
- B. We must recognize that the Holy Spirit brings revival when we seek to be filled with His presence.

C. We must begin by ensuring that we have been filled.
D. We must then continually fan into flame the gift of God.
   1. By believing the promise (John 7:37-39).
   2. By stepping out in faith and witnessing for Christ (Acts 5:32).
   3. By continually seeking God and asking to be filled (Luke 11:9-10, 13).

Conclusion and Altar Call
   1. Let us come and pray that God will fill us with the Holy Spirit.
   2. If you have never been filled before, the promise is for you. Come and let the fire be ignited in your life.
   3. If you have already received the baptism in the Holy Spirit, come and fan the flame by being refilled so that you can continue to serve Christ and witness in the power of the Holy Spirit.

~ Appendix 5 ~
TYPICAL ACTS 1:8 CONFERENCE SCHEDULES

Acts 1:8 Conference ~ Typical 4-Day Schedule

	Day 1	Day 2	Day 3	Day 4
7:30 am		Prayer 1: *Prayer for the Spirit. Prayer for the Nations*	Prayer 2: *Prayer for the Spirit. Prayer for the Nations.*	Prayer 3: *Prayer for the Spirit Prayer for the Nations.*
8:30 am		Teaching 1: *"The Holy Spirit and the Mission of God"*	Teaching 5: *"Planting the Spirit-empowered Missionary Church"*	Teaching 9: *"Pentecost and the Next Generation"*
9:15 am		Teaching 2: *"Spirit Baptism Revisited"*	Teaching 6: *"Leading a Church into Pentecostal Revival"*	Teaching 10: *"Women and Pentecostal Revival"*
10:00 am			Break	
10:30 am		Teaching 3: *"What It Means to Be Pentecostal"*	Teaching 7: *"How to Preach on the Baptism in the Holy Spirit"*	Teaching 11: *"The Pentecostal Bible School"*
11:15 am		Teaching 4: *"Prayer and Pentecostal Revival"*	Teaching 8: *"Praying with Believers to Receive the Holy Spirit"*	Teaching 12: *"The Pentecostal Leader"*
12:00 pm		Strategy 1: Assessment: *"Where Are We Now?"*	Strategy 2: Goals: *"Where Does God Want Us to Be?"*	Strategy 3: Strategy: *"What Must We Do to Get There?"*
1:00 pm			Lunch	
2:00 pm		Free Time		Strategy 4: Leaders: *"Developing the Acts 1:8 Declaration"*
5:30 pm			Dinner	
7:00 pm	Keynote Address	Holy Spirit Service	Holy Spirit Service	Commitment Service

Acts 1:8 Conference ~ Typical 5-Day Schedule

	Day 1	Day 2	Day 3	Day 4	Day 5
7:15 am		Opening Session	Opening Session	Opening Session	Opening Session
7:30 am		Prayer 1: *Prayer for the Spirit. Prayer for the Nations.*	Prayer 2: *Prayer for the Spirit. Prayer for the Nations.*	Prayer 3: *Prayer for the Spirit. Prayer for the Nations.*	Prayer 4: *Prayer for the Spirit. Prayer for the Nations.*
8:30 am		Teaching 1: *"The Holy Spirit and the Mission of God"*	Teaching 4: *"Prayer and Pentecostal Revival"*	Teaching 7: *"How to Preach on Spirit Baptism"*	Teaching 10: *"Women and Pentecostal Revival"*
9:30 am			Break		
10:00 am		Teaching 2: *"Spirit Baptism Revisited"*	Teaching 5: *"Planting the Spirit-Empowered Missionary Church"*	Teaching 8: *"Praying with Believers to Receive the Spirit"*	Teaching 11: *"The Pentecostal Bible School*
11:00 am		Teaching 3: *"What It Means to Be Pentecostal"*	Teaching 6: *"Leading a Church into Revival"*	Teaching 9: *"Pentecost and the Next Generation"*	Teaching 12: *"The Pentecostal Leader"*
12:00 pm		Strategy 1: Assessment: *"Where Are We Now?"*	Strategy 2: Goals: *"Where Does God Want Us to Be?"*	Strategy 3: Strategy: *"What Must We Do?"*	Strategy 4: Leaders: *"Developing the Acts 1:8 Declaration"*
1:00 pm			Lunch		
2:00 pm			Free Time		
5:30 pm			Dinner		
7:00 pm	Keynote Address	Holy Spirit Service	Holy Spirit Service	Holy Spirit Service	Commitment Service

OTHER DECADE OF PENTECOST BOOKS
~ Available from the Acts in Africa Initiative ~

Power Ministry: How to Minister in the Spirit's Power (2004)
(also available in French, Portuguese, Romanian, Malagasy, Kinyarwanda, and Chichewa)

Empowered for Global Mission: A Missionary Look at the Book of Acts (2005)

From Azusa to Africa to the Nations (2005)
(also available in French, Spanish, and Portuguese)

Acts: The Spirit of God in Mission (2007)

In Step with the Spirit: Studies in the Spirit-filled Walk (2008)

The Kingdom and the Power: The Kingdom of God: A Pentecostal Interpretation (2009)

Experiencing the Spirit: A Study of the Work of the Spirit in the Life of the Believer (2009)

Teaching in the Spirit (2009)

Power Encounter: Ministering in the Power and Anointing of the Holy Spirit: Revised (2009)
(also available in Kiswahili)

You Can Minister in God's Power: A Guide for Spirit-filled Disciples (2009)

The Spirit of God in Mission: A Vocational Commentary on the Book of Acts (2011)

Proclaiming Pentecost: 100 Sermon Outlines on the Power of the Holy Spirit (2011) (Available in French, Spanish, Portuguese, Amharic, Swahili, Moore, Chichewa, and Kirundi)

Globalizing Pentecostal Missions in Africa (2011) (Also available in French)

The 1:8 Promise of Jesus: The Key to World Harvest (2012)

Proclaiming Christ to the Nations: 100 Sermon Outlines on Spirit-Empowered Mission (2017)

The New Testament Strategy of the Spirit: An Acts 1:8 Model for 21st Century Church Planting (2017)

Encountering God's Missionary Spirit: A Missional Study of the Holy Spirit (2018)

Interceding for the Nations: 100 Sermon Outlines on Missional Prayer (2018)

The above books are available from
AIA Publications
580-A West Central Street
Springfield, MO, 65802, USA
E-mail: ActsinAfrica@agmd.org

www.ingramcontent.com/pod-product-compliance
Lightning Source LLC
Chambersburg PA
CBHW061645040426
42446CB00010B/1591